THIS BOOK BELONGS TO

Light and Film

Human Behavior
The Art of Sewing
The Old West
The Emergence of Man
The American Wilderness
The Time-Life Encyclopedia of Gardening
Life Library of Photography
This Fabulous Century
Foods of the World
Time-Life Library of America
Time-Life Library of Art
Great Ages of Man
Life Science Library
The Life History of the United States
Time Reading Program
Life Nature Library
Life World Library
Family Library:
 The Time-Life Book of the Family Car
 The Time-Life Family Legal Guide
 The Time-Life Book of Family Finance

LIFE LIBRARY OF PHOTOGRAPHY

Light and Film

BY THE EDITORS OF TIME-LIFE BOOKS

TIME-LIFE BOOKS, NEW YORK

ON THE COVER: Three elements make up basic tools of the photographic process: light, represented by a 300-watt bulb; a sensitive material, here a segment of 35mm film; and one of the photographer's means of controlling the interaction of the two, a 10-zone gray scale used to translate the tones of the natural world into a manageable range of gray shades in a photograph.

Contents

Valuable aid was provided by these individuals and departments of Time Inc.: TIME-LIFE Photo Lab, George Karas, Herbert Orth; Editorial Production, Norman Airey; Library, Benjamin Lightman; Picture Collection, Doris O'Neil; Photo Equipment Supervisor, Albert Schneider; TIME-LIFE News Service, Murray J. Gart; Correspondents Elisabeth Kraemer and Renee Houle (Bonn), Maria Vincenza Aloisi (Paris), Margot Hapgood (London), Ann Natanson (Rome), Traudl Lessing (Vienna), Mary Johnson (Stockholm), Robert Kroon and Alex des Fontaines (Geneva), Martha Haymaker (Los Angeles).

Once a photographer has a camera in his hands he comes up against a formidable array of technical and esthetic choices. Which film to use? How should he light the scene—with natural illumination, flash or floodlights? How should lighting angles be fixed relative to the camera for pleasing results? What f-stop and shutter speed will capture the minute detail and subtly shaded tones that a fine photograph needs?

Even an experienced photographer is often hard put to answer these questions confidently. The reason they seem so complex is that all are interrelated.

A decision on illumination always affects exposure, and the choice of film may change the other decisions. The questions also seem (or sometimes have been made to seem) mysterious because they all involve that remarkable physical quantity, light, and its reactions with the more substantial materials of the world—and most particularly with certain compounds of silver on the surface of photographic film.

The mystery disappears and the complexities begin to fall in place when the basic facts about light are understood. This volume in the LIFE Library of Photography deals with the nature of light; the evolution of modern film since the early discoveries of light's effect on sensitive substances; the types of film now available and their uses; light meters and their operation in the determination of accurate exposure; sources of artificial light; and the creation of pleasing light patterns. These topics cover the basic problems faced in taking a photograph. By exploring them in orderly fashion this book shows how the technical objectives of a "good" negative can be combined with the esthetic aims of an outstanding picture.

The Editors

Light and the Photographer **1**

KEN KAY: *Image of apple formed through lens of sectioned camera, 1969*

How Light Acts

Anybody who is old enough to take pictures understands that photography depends on light. Obviously, the film is exposed by the light that enables the eyes to see. But the dependence of photography on light goes far deeper than that and takes forms that are not nearly so obvious, for the character and quality of a picture can be altered by the character and quality of the light. The source of the light matters—the sun makes different pictures from those incandescent bulbs do (and fluorescent lights give results that are yet again different). The color of the light—and all light is colored even though the human eye seldom notices—affects not only color pictures but black-and-white ones too. Material substances—clothing, walls, a lake surface —react with light and alter its reaction with photographic film. Even the very air we breathe, invisible though it is, may have marked effects on photographs—effects that vary with the time of day.

Many of these influences of light on photographs are at first surprising. What you see with your eyes is not what you get with the camera. The explanation lies in the nature of photographic film. It does not work like the light-sensitive retina of the eye, and more important, it lacks the brain that interprets retinal signals to complete the act of "seeing." These discrepancies can ruin a picture for the unwary photographer—or create startling effects for the photographer who deliberately takes advantage of them. The most common example is the color transparency shot indoors with "outdoor" type film; it comes out with an all-over red tinge. The reason: light from ordinary incandescent bulbs is redder than daylight and the color film records it as it is while human sight does not (the brain automatically counterbalances the reddish color of the illumination).

When black-and-white film is used, the influences of the quality of light are subtler. All ordinary black-and-white films are sensitive to some light the eye cannot see and they are also more sensitive to blue-colored light and less sensitive to red-colored light than the eye is. In a photograph of a landscape, for example, a deep blue sky can turn out a blank white and a pale red flower may have blossoms almost as dark as its leaves. These departures from what seems natural to the eye can be compensated for—or deliberately emphasized—if the photographer understands a few basic facts about light and its reactions with the material substances of the world.

Light is usually described as a form of energy, and it is indeed a kind of electromagnetic energy little different from radio waves, television signals, heat and X-rays. All are made up of waves that spread, bend, interfere with one another and react with obstacles much in the manner of waves in water. But if you ask a physicist what light is, he may answer that it, together with all its electromagnetic relatives, is really a form of matter, little different from substantial things such as houses. Like them, it is made up of individual par-

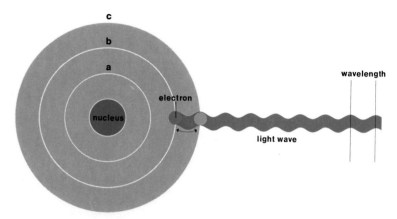

Light originates inside an atom such as the hydrogen atom diagrammed above, when one of the atom's components, an electron, oscillates in a way that is symbolized as a back and forth movement between two positions. This oscillation begins with the absorption of energy from outside the atom. Some absorbed energy goes to increase the energy content of the electron, a jump in energy that is represented as a shift of the electron from its location within the atom (orbit b) to another location (orbit c). But the higher energy levels—the orbits farther from the atom's nucleus—are less stable. The electron, like a ball lifted to a precarious spot on a narrow shelf, quickly drops back to a lower level (orbit b). The energy that is lost in this change appears as a light wave, and the wavelength of the light (marked off by parallel lines on the drawing of the waves) is established by the difference in energy between the two orbits. In the case of the hydrogen atom, the electron movement indicated produces light with a wavelength the eye senses as red.

ticles. The light particles, called photons, travel in streams in much the same way as droplets of water pouring from a hose; when a photon hits something it delivers a noticeable jolt, just as water droplets do.

There seems to be a paradox here. Can light be both energy and matter, wave and particle? The answer is yes and the reasons are not complicated. All energy is a form of matter; Einstein's famous equation $E=mc^2$ (E referring to energy and m to the mass of matter) is one indication of this fact. What is more, all matter has some characteristics of waves and some characteristics of particles. The wave characteristics of ordinary matter such as houses are rarely discernible and can generally be ignored; ordinary matter usually acts as if it were made up of particles. When it comes to the kind of matter we call light, however, the situation is quite different. Light's wave characteristics are predominant in many instances—and in yet other instances the particle characteristics reveal themselves. When light reacts with photographic film, for example, it acts like a particle: a photon strikes a molecule of silver bromide or silver iodide and partially disrupts it to make the exposure *(pages 124-125)*. But in the majority of the phenomena involved in photography, light can be described as acting like a wave, and most discussions of light in this book will refer to light waves rather than to photons.

There are three major characteristics of a light wave that concern photographers: (1) its intensity, which is related to the height of the wave crests and indirectly determines brightness of the light; (2) the wavelength, which depends on the distance between crests and largely determines color; and (3) its polarization, the angular orientation of the crests, which can be exploited for special photographic purposes. All three characteristics are influenced by what happens when light waves interact with ordinary substances: air, metal and glass surfaces, clouds, photographic filters. It is this light-matter reaction, beginning with the actual generation of a light wave inside an atom in the sun or a light bulb *(opposite),* that creates all the effects we see—and the sometimes quite different effects we photograph.

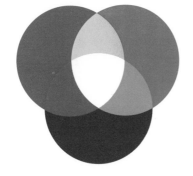

Any color can be simulated by mixing light waves of red, green and blue of varying intensities. Each hue is determined by its dominating wavelength and mixed wavelengths combine visually. Thus red plus green combine to produce yellow. All three make white.

The Electromagnetic Spectrum

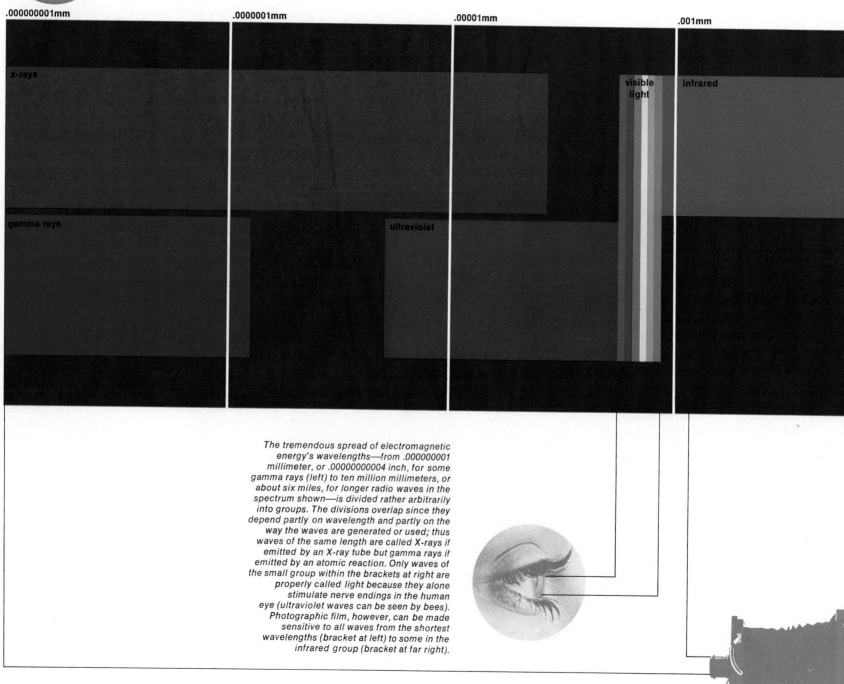

.000000001mm   .0000001mm   .00001mm   .001mm

x-rays

visible light

infrared

gamma rays

ultraviolet

The tremendous spread of electromagnetic energy's wavelengths—from .000000001 millimeter, or .00000000004 inch, for some gamma rays (left) to ten million millimeters, or about six miles, for longer radio waves in the spectrum shown—is divided rather arbitrarily into groups. The divisions overlap since they depend partly on wavelength and partly on the way the waves are generated or used; thus waves of the same length are called X-rays if emitted by an X-ray tube but gamma rays if emitted by an atomic reaction. Only waves of the small group within the brackets at right are properly called light because they alone stimulate nerve endings in the human eye (ultraviolet waves can be seen by bees). Photographic film, however, can be made sensitive to all waves from the shortest wavelengths (bracket at left) to some in the infrared group (bracket at far right).

10mm   1,000mm   100,000mm   10,000,000mm

radio waves

it seems strange to think of light waves as being almost the same as radio waves, and yet the only physical difference between them is their length. Radio waves are the longest among the broad range of electromagnetic energy waves listed above, with wavelengths as great as six miles. At the other extreme of the electromagnetic spectrum, gamma rays, produced by disintegrating atoms of radioactive elements, have wavelengths of less than approximately .000000004 inch. The visible light waves are a very small group near the middle of the spectrum with wavelengths ranging from .000016 to .000028 inch.

Within the narrow range of visible light, each individual wavelength is emitted by the sun, but greenish wavelengths are emitted in greater intensity than are the others. This mixture registers in the brain as white. But other sources of light balance their wavelengths in different ways. Electronic flash tubes and fluorescent lamps emit light that may be made up of a relatively small number of distinct wavelengths —a mixture of a few distinct colors; unless these wavelengths combine to simulate sunlight (as they do in many flash units), they produce unnatural results in color photographs. Incandescent bulbs emit a range of wavelengths, as the sun does, but the range is an unbalanced one, containing more of the long wavelengths (red colors) than it does of the short ones (blue colors).

The wavelength balance is dependent on temperature; the sun's temperature cannot be matched by incandescent filaments, and they cannot produce as many short wavelengths as the sun. The resulting reddish cast in their light must be counterbalanced for color pictures and allowed for in black-and-white photographs.

But even sunlight is not always what it seems. It includes wavelengths that are not visible light, yet do affect film. And any of its wavelengths, visible or invisible, may be absorbed, separated, re-mixed and re-emitted on their way through the air to the earth—and to the film in the back of a camera.

The Earth's Atmospheric Screen

Before there was life on earth, nearly all the sun's electromagnetic waves managed to reach the surface of the earth at one time or another. With life came a new kind of atmosphere, which now screens out most of the solar wavelengths shorter than visible light (which is fortunate since short waves can damage human tissue). The way and the degree to which the other wavelengths are able to get through depends on the atmosphere's content of carbon dioxide, smoke, dust, clouds, moisture and even on the time of day —with effects on photographic film that are sometimes annoying, sometimes surprising, sometimes beautiful.

The atmosphere screens out short wavelengths because of the way they react with matter. When short wavelengths strike molecules in air they release some of their energies, which are converted to another form. In many cases, they energize the molecules' electrons, causing them to jump to higher energy levels; when these electrons fall back they release energy that eventually takes the form of heat. Short wavelengths have then been converted into a different form of energy—they have been absorbed.

This happens only to the shortest wavelengths. Those that are not absorbed in this way include (a) a few too short to be seen, (b) all those in the visible spectrum and (c) many of those too long to be seen. The shortest of the invisible rays that get through the atmosphere in any quantity are in the group called ultraviolet. These affect all ordinary films (color as well as black and white) in the same way visible light does. Among the longer wavelengths that are invisible is the group called the infrared—they have wavelengths just longer than the deepest visible red. These infrared rays are detected by special film and prove very useful in photography. Infrared film can be used to take pictures through a layer of clouds, since many infrared waves are not absorbed by cloud particles. Needing no visible light, such film—when exposed to infrared waves—can take pictures in the dark (to trap a thief) or in dim light (to photograph a church wedding). And infrared film records natural objects, which reflect infrared differently than they do visible light, in some quite unnatural but surprisingly beautiful tones *(pages 148-149).*

Not all the waves that penetrate the atmosphere slip through unaffected. They, too, give up energy to molecules in air, but not in a way that causes energy-level jumps. When the energy is released, it is often altered in some way —in the direction of travel, the angle of undulation or in wavelengths. Since wavelength affects color, it is this re-shaping of transmitted waves that gives sky, clouds and sunsets their colors.

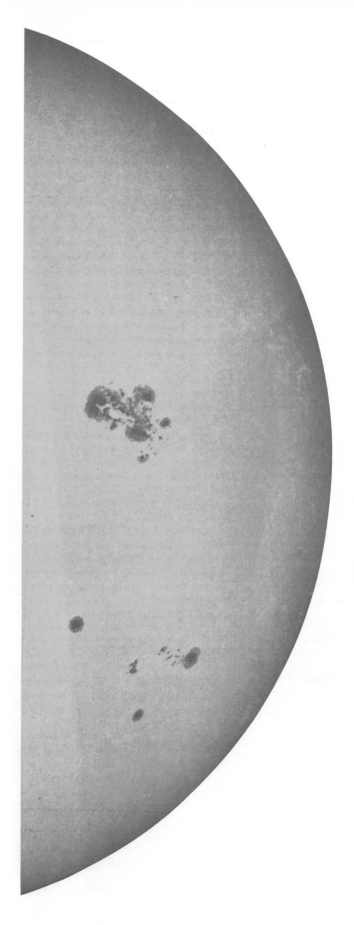

ultravi

b

gre

infra

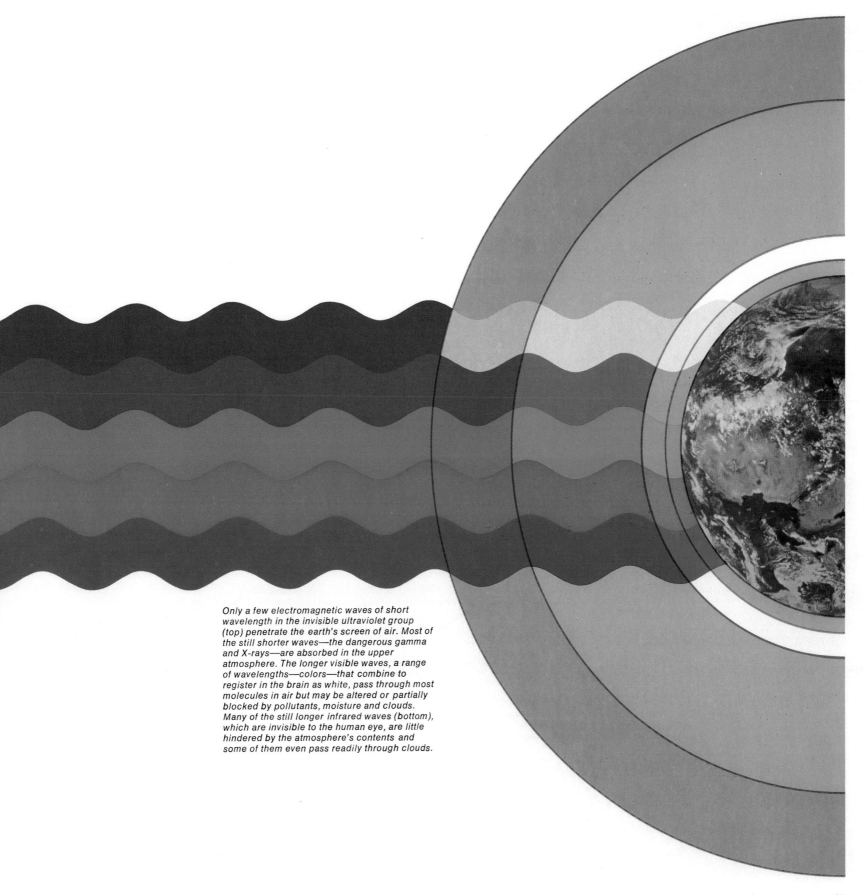

Only a few electromagnetic waves of short wavelength in the invisible ultraviolet group (top) penetrate the earth's screen of air. Most of the still shorter waves—the dangerous gamma and X-rays—are absorbed in the upper atmosphere. The longer visible waves, a range of wavelengths—colors—that combine to register in the brain as white, pass through most molecules in air but may be altered or partially blocked by pollutants, moisture and clouds. Many of the still longer infrared waves (bottom), which are invisible to the human eye, are little hindered by the atmosphere's contents and some of them even pass readily through clouds.

Scattering: Key to Sky Colors

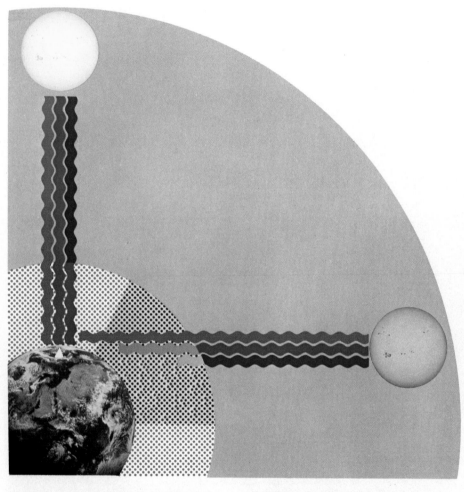

The spectacular color of the sunset at right is caused by the same phenomenon that makes the sky blue: the selective scattering of light waves by molecules of air (and very small dust and water particles). When these molecules react with light waves passing by, they affect the shorter wavelengths (bluish colors) more than the longer ones (yellow and red), bouncing them around and giving the sky its bluish tinge.

When to an observer on earth the sun appears low in the sky, near the horizon —as at sunrise and sunset—its light travels a greater distance through the atmosphere than when it is overhead *(diagram at left).* Traversing more air molecules, the light waves undergo more scattering. So many of the shorter waves are scattered that relatively few get straight through to an observer; the waves that do get through are mostly the longer yellow and red wavelengths and, therefore, the sun appears yellow-orange. Sunsets in a clear cloudless sky are generally unimpressive, but when a beam of this reddish light paints the clouds it produces spectacular displays like the one at the right.

Not only is the color of the sun when it is low in the sky different from its appearance during the rest of the day, but the quality of the overall illumination is different, too. Because more of the rays from the sun are scattered around through the atmosphere at sunrise and sunset, the balance between the brightness of sky light and of direct sun rays becomes more even than it is at midday. The sky light brightens shadows and softens the contrast between light and dark areas to create the delicate illumination photographers prize.

The distance the sun's light travels through the atmosphere, changing with the time of day, causes its alterations in hue. At noon the sun is directly over an observer standing at the point indicated by the arrow and its rays pierce the narrow band of atmosphere perpendicularly. The molecules in air scatter more of the short blue waves, but less of the longer green or the still longer red ones, which pass through. The sun then appears yellow (because a combination of green and red waves looks yellow) and the sky is blue. At sunset, the light reaches the observer obliquely, traveling through much more atmosphere. It has encountered more molecules and more scattering takes place—so reducing the proportion of short (blue and green) wavelengths that the longer reddish ones predominate; the sky then takes on a red tinge and the sun looks a bright yellow-orange.

HARALD SUND: *Sunset, Rocky Mountain National Park, Colorado,* 1969

The Varieties of Reflection

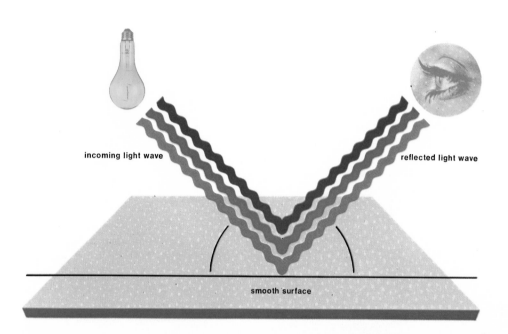

incoming light wave   reflected light wave

smooth surface

Light waves bounce off a smooth surface as a ball bounces off a wall: the angle of incidence equals the angle of reflection. All the reflected waves remain organized like the incoming ones, and the eye sees the light bulb as a reflected image. If the surface is rough, however, some waves hit and bounce at one angle, others at different angles; the reflected waves become disorganized and no image can be seen.

Light coming from the sun is unpolarized—the waves undulate at all angles, as indicated by the light and dark red waves below. They can be polarized—made to undulate at one angle, as indicated by the single pale red wave. This can happen when light waves are reflected at certain angles by such nonmetallic substances as glass and water. The part of the light that continues through the substance remains essentially unpolarized. Metals are different—their electrons have a different arrangement that does not cause reflected light waves to be polarized.

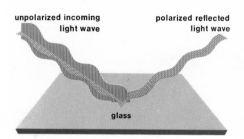

unpolarized incoming   polarized reflected
light wave   light wave

glass

Any smooth surface—polished metal or a highland pool *(right)*—bounces light waves to create a reflected image *(diagram at left above)*. Metals send the incoming waves back out essentially unchanged, which is why they make good mirrors. But certain nonmetallic substances such as diamonds, glass and water have a different electron arrangement and reflect differently in ways important to photographers. Their electrons are interrelated, each layer with the one behind, so that light energy striking the surface electrons is partially passed along to those behind; the result is a dim reflection. When a nonmetal's electrons are so closely interrelated, the waves they release can undulate at the same angle *(left).* Even this dim reflection can be killed by a thin coating of another material—the antireflection coating used on camera lenses. The electrons in the coating reverse the reflected waves and pass them, too, to electrons in the rear.

HARALD SUND: *Sunrise over Highland Pool, Mount Evans, Colorado,* 1969

Bending Waves by Refraction

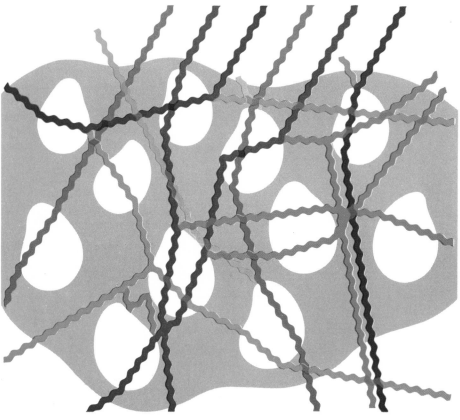

A substance composed of transparent particles —such as clouds or sugar—is diffusely luminous instead of transparent because of the way light is reflected at the particle surfaces and refracted, or bent, inside the particles. If the light reaching the particles (top) is a mixture of wavelengths—which gives white light—a similar mixture emerges (bottom) with the directions of its waves altered (hence the diffusion).

Clouds are transparent water droplets —yet they usually look the way they do at right, a diffuse white instead of transparent. Refraction, the bending of light, is one reason.

When the light waves enter or leave a droplet they bend so that they zigzag through the cloud and emerge in many directions. Reflections at the droplet surfaces also change waves' directions, adding to the disorganization and giving the cloud a diffuse white look.

Glass also bends light by refraction, but does not look white—unless it is finely powdered. When it is solid, as in a camera lens, it produces only a few controlled changes of direction and the light waves remain organized.

HARALD SUND: *Landscape with Clouds, vicinity of Hartsel, Colorado,* 1969

How Filters Work

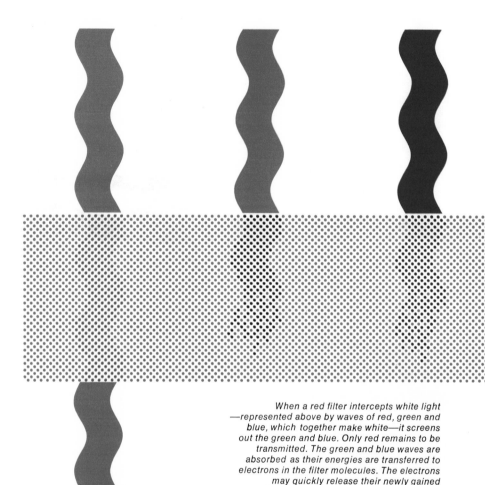

The man-sized glass discs at the right, which are components of a piece of modern sculpture, work just like the filters a photographer places over the lens of his camera to control the film's rendition of colored objects *(pages 176-177)*. The discs achieve their multicolored effect by allowing certain wavelengths of light to pass through them while absorbing others *(diagram at left)*. Daylight—the mixture of all colors forming white light—from outside the gallery window appears variously yellow, red, blue or black, depending on which filter, or combination of filters, it is seen through.

A segment of the edge of the blue disc at right looks black because it overlaps the red behind it. Between them they absorb all colors and allow no light to pass. Yet the yellow disc, a thin sliver of which shows at the left of the picture, does not affect the color of the overlapping red disc—the red disc still looks red. Their absorption provides the explanation. Yellow glass absorbs mainly blue and transmits yellow, green and red (a combination that the brain registers as yellow). Since little red is absorbed by the yellow disc, it does not alter the appearance of the red disc in front of it.

Which wavelengths a filter absorbs are determined by molecular structure. If an orbit exists that an electron can jump to when struck by light of a particular wavelength, that wavelength is usually absorbed. Energy levels can be matched to almost any wavelength by applying modern chemical methods, and filters can be compounded to absorb a few wavelengths, a broad range of wavelengths or even several separate wavelengths in the spectrum. □

When a red filter intercepts white light —represented above by waves of red, green and blue, which together make white—it screens out the green and blue. Only red remains to be transmitted. The green and blue waves are absorbed as their energies are transferred to electrons in the filter molecules. The electrons may quickly release their newly gained energies, but usually in the form of heat rather than in that of light. The warmth produced in this manner can actually be felt after such a filter has been exposed to white light for a time.

JAN LUKAS: *Sculpture, Expo '67, Montreal,* 1967

How Photographers Exploit Light

The hard, vertical line of white light that pierces the shadows in Charles Harbutt's photograph at the right demands attention. It draws the eye directly into the picture and like an arrow points to a young boy's hands pressed flat against a wall. The light and the hands convey the photographer's thought: the boy is blind; he has discovered light in the only way he can, through touch.

This picture is one of a series Harbutt made of children at The Lighthouse in New York City, an institution for the blind. Harbutt had noticed, after observing him for several days, that this painfully deprived boy used his hands to feel for the warmth created by the warm rays of the sunlight that threaded the narrow space between two buildings each afternoon at about the same time. It was the only light needed for exposure, and it made Harbutt's picture.

Like Harbutt, the photographers who took the pictures on the pages that follow used the physical characteristics of light to dramatize reality: direct sunlight for a hard, graphic image, hazily diffused daylight for a mysterious, romantic quality, directional light to accent a figure or emphasize form. They employed its qualities deliberately; no photograph shown is a lucky shot. Each results from a conscious awareness of what light can do in a photograph.

It is common for a serious photographer to spend a great deal of time at this, experimenting with light just as he does with cameras and film. George Krause is one who, like several other outstanding professionals, spent the early part of his career making all his pictures on overcast days, when the illumination was diffuse. When he felt he had mastered the use of such lighting he turned to scenes with harsher contrasts of shadow and brightness—with the stunning results shown on page 38. Such concentration on one particular aspect of light helps a photographer learn to "see" light—i.e., to visualize the differences that changes in illumination will make. With this educated and heightened sense of perception he can make a picture live up to the original Greek meaning of the word photography: "light writing." Shadows, reflections, patterns of light, even the light source itself may become the heart of a composition in which solid objects are incidental and light is the theme.

CHARLES HARBUTT: *Blind Boy, New York City*, c. 1960

27

Making the Source Unify the Picture

ROBERT GNANT: *Shepherd, Switzerland, c.1960*

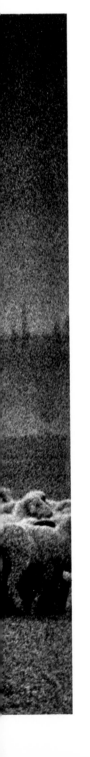

IRWIN DERMER: *The Whisperers, England,* 1966

Just as the sun blinds us if we look directly into it, any light source included in a composition tends to overwhelm the subject it illuminates. But when a balance can be struck, the picture acquires a special sense of completeness. We not only see the view but understand why it looks that way, as in Robert Gnant's photograph of a shepherd with his flock by moonlight *(opposite),* or in Irwin Dermer's portrait of the English actress Dame Edith Evans as a lonely old woman in the movie *The Whisperers,* her world encompassed by a tea table, her sun an electric bulb.

Setting a Mood

RAY METZKER: *Alley, Philadelphia,* 1964

Light coming directly from a single source—the sun, a spotlight—is harsh, creating bright planes and deep shadows, as in Ray Metzker's photograph of a truck in a city alley. It is a picture of absolutes; detail fades in the deep blacks and bright whites. The composition is bold, graphic and without emotion. A face photographed with such light coming directly into it is more likely to appear as a sketch than as a portrait, since broad generalities are stressed rather than the detail that defines personality.

Reflected or diffused light—from the walls of a room, from the sky on an overcast day—is soft. It fills in shadows and plays down contours. Neal Slavin's study of an amusement park lying dormant in winter, with all the people, fun and excitement gone, shows a scene almost faded from view; the soft light that filters through a snowstorm seems to come from everywhere and nowhere.

NEAL SLAVIN: *Coney Island, New York,* 1964

Isolating the Image

HARRY CALLAHAN: *Wabash Avenue, Chicago,* 1958

There is nothing wrong with the old rule of putting the sun at your back when making a snapshot. It ensures maximum illumination of the subject. But the directional characteristics of light can be exploited in subtler ways. In the Chicago street scene above, Harry Callahan has set his camera so that the bright sun high on his left and slightly in front of him picks out the figure of a woman from a dark wall behind her. In Leonard Freed's picture of Hasidic Jews at a wedding party *(right),* the interest lies in the individual expression on each man's face and in the placement of his hands—the very elements emphasized by the bright light that floods in horizontally from the left.

LEONARD FREED: *Jewish Wedding Party, New York*, 1960

Revealing Form and Texture

EDWARD WESTON: *Church Door, Hornitos, California,* 1940

Light falling obliquely across the front of an old church celebrates the natural texture of weatherbeaten wood in Edward Weston's photograph at the left. Weston, who invariably relied on natural light for illumination, on several occasions waited for hours for the exact balancing of quality, direction and intensity that achieved the effect he sought. The problem is more easily solved in the studio, where oblique light can be precisely controlled to convey the reality of surfaces and shapes. At the right, Pierre Jousson has aimed a single spot-light to brush the surface of a nude model, creating a contrasting pattern of lights and darks that gently defines the female form.

PIERRE JOUSSON: *Nude, Lausanne, Switzerland,* 1963

A Fresh View in Reflections

The Po River had flooded and in its still waters the stark trunks of poplars on a tree farm were doubled in reflection —to photographer Harold Miller Null it seemed an "interplay of lines and angles that imparts a Gothic feeling to these avenues of trees. . . . A few days later if you passed by you would see the trees cut, the water receding, the whole thing looking entirely different—like any muddy, dirty field anywhere."

Rather than Null's sense of another time, a transformation of space is created by reflection in William Garnett's aerial photograph of Buena Vista Lake in southern California. The heavy, bold image of the sun is seen mirrored in the lake surface. But the flight of snow geese is not reflected. The birds are pictured directly, flying beneath the camera plane and above the sun image —turning topsy-turvy our normal view of them. The pattern is multiplied in complexity by shadows visible on the lake surface, and again as ghostly echoes off the shallow lake bottom. The faint, blurred dots in the upper left-hand corner of the picture are shadows cast by another flock of birds flying at a much higher altitude.

HAROLD MILLER NULL: *Winter Reflection, Italy,* 1961

WILLIAM GARNETT: *Snow Geese over Water, Buena Vista Lake, California*, c. 1953

Composition in Shadows

GEORGE KRAUSE: *The Shadow, Seville, Spain,* 1963

Shadows of two women, one discovered at dawn on a street in Seville, Spain, the other created in a studio in Prague, Czechoslovakia, carry the weight of these two pictures. The women themselves become almost incidental to the composition. In the photograph above, horizontal early light casts such a looming shadow for George Krause that he captured what seems to be the image of a dark secret following the woman, its sinister implication enhanced by the bent carriage of her head. In Frantisek Drtikol's picture *(opposite),* a single studio bulb was placed behind paper tubes to create the arching shadows that complete the composition.

FRANTISEK DRTIKOL: *Nude, Prague, Czechoslovakia,* c. 1920

Patterns in Brightness

KENNETH JOSEPHSON: *Chicago*, 1961

Shadows made the pictures on the two previous pages. Here, light reverses roles: its presence rather than its absence paints the patterns that the eye seizes upon. Kenneth Josephson snapped his shutter at the exact moment four pedestrians were spotlighted by the random shafts of sunlight pen- etrating the gloom under a Chicago el *(above).* In Lars Werner Thieme's un- usual photograph of a German organ grinder *(opposite),* the pattern of sun- light infiltrating a Munich arcade pro- vides the picture's substance, more solid seeming than the pavement and the wall it presses against.

LARS WERNER THIEME: *Ash Wednesday, Munich, Germany, 1967*

Creating Mystery

RONALD MESAROS: *Vesta, Topanga Canyon, California,* 1966

The fog was rolling in from the Pacific Ocean on the afternoon that Ronald Mesaros took a friend, his 35mm Minolta and his Doberman pinscher, Vesta, for a walk in the hills above Los Angeles. The light, filtering through the fog, was dull and nondirectional. It was barely strong enough to produce detail in the face of the girl who had accompanied Mesaros, but not sufficient to do more than outline the shape of his black dog. Taking advantage of this unusual contrast, Mesaros produced the disquieting photograph above—a smiling girl, seemingly oblivious of the sinister, featureless silhouette looming up behind her. The mood of the picture, one of tension, mystery and imminent danger, would surely dissolve in the glare of bright sunlight. ☐

The Evolution of Film **2**

PHOTOGRAPHER UNKNOWN: *Studio of the Photographer Bourgeois, Paris*, c. 1870

45

The Inventors of Photography

After completing a lecture at the Sorbonne one day in 1827, Jean Dumas, an outstanding chemist of the period, was approached by an obviously perturbed woman who introduced herself as "the wife of Daguerre, the painter." Her husband, she said, was "possessed." He was convinced he could make permanent pictures from the fleeting images produced by a lens. "I'm afraid he is out of his mind," she said. "Do you, as a man of science, think it can ever be done, or is he mad?"

"In our present state of knowledge, it cannot be done," Dumas replied, "but I cannot say it will always remain impossible, nor set the man down as mad who seeks to do it."

Dumas was not merely pacifying a worried woman; he had good reason not to dismiss the idea of recording permanent images with light. As a chemist, he undoubtedly knew that certain silver compounds were reactive to light —as early as the 17th Century, an Italian scientist, Angelo Sala, had reported that "when you expose powdered silver nitrate to the sun, it turns black as ink"—and that men had already recorded short-lived pictures with these compounds. The unsolved and enormously difficult problem was how to "fix" the recorded pattern, halting the reaction with light so that the picture would not fade away.

In 1727, a hundred years before Madame Daguerre talked with Dumas, Johann Heinrich Schulze, professor of medicine at the University of Altdorf in Germany, made the first of these ephemeral pictures. One day, as part of an experiment that had nothing to do with light images, he stood a flask containing a silver nitrate mixture in sunlight; when he inspected it a few minutes later, he found the part of the solution that had received the direct rays of the sun had turned a dark violet, while the remainder of the mixture retained its original whitish color. When he shook the bottle, the violet disappeared.

Intrigued by this phenomenon, Schulze pasted paper stencils on the flask and faced them directly toward the sun. When he later removed the stencils, there, outlined by the surrounding darkened sediment, were the whitish patterns—i.e., negative silhouettes—of the light-blocking slips of paper. But was it the sun's light or its heat that caused the unshaded chemicals to darken? To answer that question, Schulze placed another container of the mixture in a hot, dark oven. It was not affected; obviously light had caused the change. The silhouettes were soon gone, however. Within a comparatively short time, just the reflected daylight in the room darkened them to the same shade as the surrounding sediment.

In the early 19th Century, Thomas Wedgwood, the youngest son of Josiah Wedgwood, the famous British pottery manufacturer, made similar experiments with similarly tantalizing results. He made some attempts to record the natural images created by a lens in a camera obscura, the ancient device that artists used, to cast a picture of a scene on a glass viewing screen. The results, however, were so poor that he concentrated on making silhouettes like Schulze's, placing leaves and insect wings on silver sensitized white paper or white leather and exposing them to the sun. Like Schulze, he achieved negative images. Wedgwood tried many ways to make these silhouettes permanent, but nothing worked. As soon as light, however subdued, struck the images, they began to darken like the rest of the coating.

Schulze and Wedgwood were on the right track. The silver atom's unique properties enable it to form compounds and crystals that respond in delicate, controllable ways to the energy of light waves *(pages 124-125).* Over the following century many different men from a variety of callings—not only scientists but artists, printers, soldiers, country squires, even clergymen —helped to develop silver-based materials into the practical roll film that has made photography everyman's art form. But oddly enough, silver played no part at all in the first permanent pictures that can be called true photographs, made in about 1824 by Joseph-Nicéphore Niepce, a gentleman inventor and lithographer living in Chalon-sur-Saône in central France. They were produced with, of all things, asphalt.

Niepce began his experiments partly because of a business need. In the lithographic process of printing as it was then practiced, copies were produced from a flat stone surface that had a design transferred onto it, much as in printing from woodcuts or engravings. To produce lithographs of a line drawing, for example, the drawing had first to be copied (in reverse) on the stone surface. Niepce's son, Isidore, had done this work, but he had been called for his tour of duty with the army. Niepce had no talent for draftsmanship and he decided to devise an automatic method of copying line drawings onto his lithographic stones.

Niepce knew that a certain kind of asphalt, called bitumen of Judea, hardened when exposed to light. He dissolved this asphalt in lavender oil, a solvent used in varnishes, and then coated a sheet of pewter with the mixture. Face down on the coated surface he placed a line drawing that had been oiled to make it translucent and then exposed the plate and illustration to sunlight. The sun hardened the asphalt wherever the blank areas of the drawing permitted light to shine through onto the plate, but in the sections shielded from the light by the black lines of the drawing, the coating remained soft and soluble. After removing the oiled drawing, Niepce washed the plate with lavender oil. This removed the soft soluble asphalt that had not been struck by light. The parts of the plate that duplicated the black sections of the original drawing were cleaned down to the pewter base and etched with acid in order to make an incised copy. The incised lines held the ink to make the print. Niepce called his new process heliogravure—from the

Greek *helios* for "sun" and the French *gravure* for "engraving." He made a number of heliographic plates of drawings of the Virgin, the Infant Jesus, Saint Joseph and other subjects, but a more exciting use soon occurred to him: why not put one of his asphalt-coated plates inside a camera obscura and make pictures directly from nature? Carefully placing a plate at the back of the camera, he aimed its lens through an open window at his courtyard and left it there all day. When the plate was removed and washed in lavender oil, it bore a barely decipherable view of roofs and chimneys. In an attempt to get a better image and reduce the impractically long exposure time, Niepce tried a number of other light-sensitive materials, including a plate of silver-coated copper. The results, however, were not encouraging.

Word of Niepce's work filtered through France and one day he received a letter from a stranger, a Parisian named Louis Daguerre. Daguerre wrote that he, too, was experimenting with the recording of images and suggested an exchange of information. Niepce's reply was guarded. Darkly suspicious, he wrote to a business associate in Paris in February 1827 to inquire about Daguerre: "This gentleman, having been informed, I do not know to what extent, of the object of my researches, wrote to me last year . . . to let me know that for a long time he had occupied himself with the same object and he asked me if I had been more fortunate than he in my results. However, if he is to be believed, he has already obtained very astonishing results; notwithstanding this, he requested me to tell him first whether I thought the matter was possible at all. I do not want to deceive you, Monsieur, that a seeming incoherence of his ideas has caused me not to tell him too much. . . . Will you be good enough to send me your personal information on Daguerre and your opinion of him."

The reply was moderately reassuring. "I believe," wrote Niepce's associate, "he has a rare intelligence for the things that deal with machines and lighting effects; I know he has occupied himself for a long time with perfecting the camera obscura, but I do not know the object of his work. . . ."

In August of that year, Niepce was in Paris and met Daguerre for the first time. Except for their mutual interest in recording images with the camera obscura, the men seemingly had little in common. Niepce, then 64, had been born to the French aristocracy and was a quiet, reserved man with a sound classical education and an excellent background in science. The French Revolution had sharply reduced his wealth, but he continued to receive enough money from the family estate to enable him to devote most of his time to scientific pursuits. Before he became interested in his photographic process, he and his brother, Claude, had spent some years dabbling with other inventions, including a method for extracting indigo dye and an internal combustion engine. Although they were successful in propelling a boat up and down the Seine and Saône Rivers with the engine, neither invention ever proved commercially feasible.

Daguerre, who was Niepce's junior by 22 years, came from a middle-class family, was largely self-educated and knew almost nothing of science but was nevertheless a remarkably talented and energetic man. Because of his skill at drawing, Daguerre had been apprenticed at the age of 16 to an architect, but he left after three years to become a painter and a stage designer for the Paris Opera. He was also one of the inventors of the enormously popular Diorama. In this spectacle, usually staged in a specially built exhibit hall, famous scenes, such as the interior of Canterbury Cathedral or panoramas of the Swiss Alps, were re-created with three-dimensional effects through the use of translucent paintings and sophisticated lighting. Among his other talents, Daguerre danced well enough to appear occasionally with the corps de ballet at the Opera and was an amateur acrobat with professional competence—tight-rope walking was his specialty.

Despite the dissimilarity in their backgrounds and characters, Niepce and Daguerre apparently liked each other at first meeting. During the next two years, they corresponded about their work and met from time to time to discuss their progress. (The ever-cautious Niepce, however, disclosed few details of his actual methods.) Then, in 1829, Niepce proposed that Daguerre become his partner and engage "in mutual work in the improvement of my heliographic process, and the various ways of applying it, taking a share in the profits that its improvements will permit us to hope for."

Daguerre quickly accepted and then visited Niepce in Chalon to learn about heliogravure and to make plans for the joint project. After Daguerre returned to Paris, the partners never saw each other again. For the next four years, they worked separately and reported on their experiments by mail. Much of their research during this period was focused on the application of iodine, the reddish nonmetallic element that had been discovered in 1811 and was found to form a very light-sensitive compound with silver. But Niepce did not live to enjoy the eventual success of their work. He died of a stroke in 1833, leaving his partner to carry on alone.

On January 7, 1839, Daguerre was finally satisfied with his new photographic process and arranged to announce it before the French Academy of Sciences. Aware of his own lack of scientific training and reluctant to submit himself to questions that might be asked by the Academy members, Daguerre requested a scientist friend to make the actual presentation for him. It was a triumph. The photographs, which the inventor called "daguerreotypes," were examined with awe and enthusiastically praised.

Reporting on the pictures, the prestigious *Journal of the Franklin Institute* of Philadelphia said that the Academy members "were particularly struck with the marvelous minuteness of detail. . . . In one representing the Pont Marie, all the minutest indentations and divisions of the ground, of the buildings, the goods lying on the wharf, even the small stones under the water, were all shown with incredible accuracy. The use of a magnifying glass revealed an infinity of other details quite undistinguishable by the naked eye."

Daguerre did not reveal details of his process for some months after its announcement and during this interval some chose to consider his pictures a fraud. A German publication, *Leipziger Stadtanzeiger,* found that Daguerre's claims affronted both German science and God, in that order: "The wish to capture evanescent reflections is not only impossible, as has been shown by thorough German investigation, but the mere desire alone, the will to do so, is blasphemy. God created man in His own image, and no man-made machine may fix the image of God." The *Stadtanzeiger* held that if such wise men of the past as Archimedes and Moses "knew nothing of mirror pictures made permanent, then one can straightway call the Frenchman Daguerre, who boasts of such unheard of things, the fool of fools."

The teapot tempest subsided when the mechanics of the process were revealed in August 1839. Daguerre had perfected a very sophisticated photographic method. His light-sensitive material was silver iodide, similar to but more effective than the compounds used by Schulze and Wedgwood. And somehow (the record is vague on this point) he had hit upon the solution to the centuries-old problem of "fixing" the picture into a permanent, fade-proof image. Daguerre discovered that a chemical now known as sodium thiosulfate—photographer's "hypo"—dissolved light-sensitive silver compounds before they had been transformed into a visible image but not afterward. Thus he could make an exposure and before any other light struck the picture bathe it in hypo to halt further action by light.

Except for the fixing step, Daguerre's process was totally different from modern photography. The daguerreotype was made on a highly polished surface of silver, plated on a copper sheet *(pages 60-61)*. It was sensitized by placing it, silver side down, over a container of iodine crystals inside a box. Rising vapor from the iodine reacted with the silver, producing the light-sensitive compound silver iodide. During exposure in the camera, the plate recorded an image that at this state was latent—a chemical change had taken place but no evidence of it was visible. To develop the image, the plate was placed, again silver side down, in another box, this one containing a dish of heated mercury at the bottom. Vapor from the mercury reacted with the exposed grains of silver iodide on the plate. Wherever light had struck the plate, mercury formed an amalgam, or alloy, with silver. This brilliantly shiny amalgam thus made up the bright areas of the image. Where no light had struck, no amalgam was formed; the unchanged silver iodide was dissolved away in sodium thiosulfate fixer, leaving there the bare metal plate, which looked black, to form the dark areas of the picture.

The sharpness and tonal range of the daguerreotype continues to be among the wonders of photography. Anyone who has examined at close range one of the many small, velvet-framed pictures exhibited in historical collections cannot help but marvel at their lifelike appearance, precisely detailed, delicately shaded and naturally luminous. The image is literally a bas-relief created by the mercury. The amount of the mercury amalgamated with silver at each point in the image varies directly with the amount of light that has struck that point on the plate and it is this very gradual build-up of amalgam that creates a seemingly infinite range of grays. The amalgam is mirrorlike in reflectivity, so that highlighted areas are unusually brilliant, while the deep, rich black of the dark sections is simply the polished silver plate, which when viewed from the proper angle reflects almost no light.

The French government quickly recognized the value of the new process and just seven months after Daguerre's announcement to the Academy, he and Niepce's son, Isidore, were awarded lifetime pensions. Soon the daguerreotype became an adjunct to historical functions. "At the opening of the railroad to Courtrai, Belgium," the British *Mining Journal* reported in 1840, ". . . the camera obscura is to be placed on an eminence commanding the royal pavillion, the locomotive engine, the train of wagons, and the major part of the cortege, and is to be brought into action exactly at the time of the delivery of the inauguration speech. A discharge of cannon is to be the signal for a general immobility, which is to last the seven minutes necessary for obtaining a good representation of all the personages present."

There was, however, criticism of the new process. While praising it as an invention "little short of miraculous," a British publication, *The Penny Cyclopedia,* complained that the highly polished surface of the daguerreotype produced a "glare offensive to the eye." The journal also found fault with the curious tendency of the plates to appear as negatives unless viewed from exactly the right angle. This meant the pictures could not be hung in frames, since "it would be necessary to take them down to look at them."

But there were other, more important disadvantages that made the daguerreotype a technological dead end in spite of its superb quality. The plate required artful polishing, sensitizing and developing, and the image was extremely delicate and required elaborate protection from abrasion. The most serious drawback of the process, however, was that each plate was unique; there was no way of producing multiple copies except by rephotographing the original.

Although the daguerreotype would continue to be made for about a decade, the process was actually obsolete when it was introduced. Photography's time had come and in England a gentleman scientist had already invented the modern photographic process. On January 25, 1839, less than three weeks after Daguerre's announcement to the French Academy, William Henry Fox Talbot appeared before the Royal Institution of Great Britain to present his negative-positive system. Talbot was a disappointed man when he gave his hastily prepared report. Daguerre's prior announcement, Talbot admitted later, "frustrated the hope with which I had pursued, during nearly five years, this long and complicated series of experiments—the hope, namely, of being the first to announce to the world the existence of the New Art—which has since been named Photography." Although Talbot could not be the first, he was determined to establish, as soon as possible, that his process was wholly independent of Daguerre's.

Talbot was fairly typical of a number of amateur scientists who graced the gentry of the early 19th Century. Born in southern England in 1800 to an upper-class family—his mother was the daughter of an earl, his father an officer in the Dragoons—Talbot received a proper education at Harrow and Trinity College, was elected a Fellow of the Royal Society for his contributions to mathematics and served briefly as a member of Parliament. He sometimes used a camera obscura to help him in sketching, one of his hobbies, and he recalled that in 1833 "the idea occurred to me—how charming it would be if it were possible to cause these natural images to imprint themselves durably and remain fixed on paper." He soon began his experiments.

Talbot's first attempts were silhouettes, produced by placing objects on light-sensitive paper and exposing them to the sun—the technique used earlier by Wedgwood. Talbot sensitized a fine grade of writing paper by dipping it into a weak mixture of salt and water, waiting for it to dry and then brushing the sheet with a silver nitrate solution. This operation was repeated several times with each sheet. But unlike Wedgwood, Talbot soon learned how to retard, if not halt completely, the fading of the image. In his experiments, he observed that sensitivity was nearly eliminated in areas of the paper where the salt concentration was excessive. He applied this discovery by dipping the exposed sheet in a concentrated salt solution. (Soon he was led to the permanent fixative that Daguerre had independently discovered, sodium thiosulfate, by his friend and fellow scientist, Sir John Herschel.)

Now Talbot carried the making of a silhouette a step further: he made a positive paper print of it. The negative silhouette—i.e., a white image of, say, a leaf, outlined by the surrounding dark areas—was placed face down on a second piece of sensitized paper. Then the two were pressed together under a pane of glass and exposed to sunlight, a procedure now known as contact printing. Light could pass through the leaf's white image on the negative and thereby create a dark image on the second sheet; meanwhile the dark areas of the negative blocked light so that the corresponding sections of the second sheet remained white. The result was a positive resembling the natural original, a dark leaf against a white background. This was the foundation for the negative-positive system of modern photography. The most important test came when Talbot applied the technique to an image recorded in a camera. After exposing a negative to an outdoor scene, he made a positive print: a recognizable picture of the scene.

With the light-sensitive coating used in these early experiments, the image could be seen forming during the exposure. Talbot simply looked at the paper under the pane of glass if he were making a silhouette, or peered through a hole in the camera if he were taking a picture, and when the negative image was sufficiently pronounced, halted the exposure. But in June 1840, about a year and a half after his appearance before the Royal Institution, Talbot announced a revolutionary advance: a new, highly sensitive negative material that recorded a latent image on paper. Nothing could be seen on this new coating after exposure, he said, but he "found that the picture existed there, although invisible; and by a chemical process . . . it was made to appear in all its perfection." Talbot called the process "calotype" from the Greek words *kalos* for "beautiful" and *typos* for "impression." (It was Talbot's friend, Sir John Herschel, who later coined the name by which the process is now known, from the Greek words *photos* for "light" and *graphos* for "drawing." Sir John was also the first to employ the words "negative" and "positive" to describe Talbot's system.)

Talbot made a number of improvements in the calotype over the next several years. By increasing the sensitivity of the coating, he was able to reduce the required exposure time, enabling him to photograph people. But there was one flaw in the paper negative, and Talbot never eliminated it completely. The fibers in the paper blocked some light during the printing operation and thus produced a soft, slightly fuzzy photograph. When the inventor began waxing his negatives to increase translucency, this distortion was almost eradicated, but the calotype's sharpness never quite matched that of the daguerreotype.

The problems of the paper negative became academic in October 1847 when Abel Niepce de Saint-Victor, an army officer and cousin of Nicéphore Niepce, appeared before the Academy of Sciences in Paris to announce his new process, one that used glass plates coated with an emulsion of a silver compound suspended in egg white. The advantages of glass over paper as a base had been apparent for some time to other experimenters; glass presented no texture problems, was uniformly transparent and chemically inert. But until Niepce de Saint-Victor used egg white, no one had found an emulsion that would hold a light-sensitive material on glass, although many sticky substances, including the slime exuded by snails, had been tried.

To prepare his emulsion, Niepce de Saint-Victor functioned as part chef and part chemist. To the egg white he added a bit of potassium iodide and then whipped the mixture until it was stiff. This froth was spread evenly on the glass plate, permitted to dry and was then made light sensitive by being dipped into a bath of acidified silver nitrate.

Photographers were not unanimously enthusiastic about the new process, however. Although it could produce pictures with excellent detail, thanks to the textureless base, the early egg-white plate was easily damaged and was no faster than the calotype; image quality varied with the relative freshness of the eggs; and the plates were heavy, clumsy to manipulate and fragile. But the demonstration of the practicality of glass as a base was to prove of enormous importance to photography. With the discovery of a far better emulsion a few years later, photographers quickly learned to live with the inconveniences and shortcomings of glass plates.

Probably nothing could have been more remote than photography in the mind of Louis Ménard, a French chemist, when he discovered in 1846 that guncotton (cellulose nitrate) would dissolve in a mixture of ether and alcohol to produce a highly viscous liquid that dried into a hard, colorless, transparent film. He called the substance "collodion." He could find no use for this odd fluid but physicians soon adopted it as a dressing for minor wounds. Applied as a liquid, collodion dried into a tough, waterproof covering that protected the damaged area and kept it clean. The idea of using collodion as a photographic emulsion was first advanced by Robert Bingham, a British chemist, in January 1850.

Coating a plate required nimble fingers, flexible wrists and practiced timing. After pouring collodion in the middle of the plate, the photographer held the glass on the edges with his fingertips and tilted it back and forth and from side to side until the surface was evenly covered. The excess collodion was poured back into its container. After being sensitized in silver nitrate, the plate was exposed while still damp and then developed immediately, for Bingham had learned that the collodion emulsion became less sensitive as it dried. Thus the process became known as "wet-plate photography."

When wet collodion plates were developed in pyrogallic acid (pyrogallol), introduced in 1851, exposure time could be reduced to as little as five seconds. Because this high speed permitted the taking of pictures never before possible, photographers were willing to put up with the tedious business of preparing the plates and the need to complete the exposure-to-development cycle while the emulsion was still wet. It was with cumbersome wet plates that Mathew Brady and his men documented the Civil War *(pages 96-103)* and William Henry Jackson photographed the American West *(pages 86-89)*.

Professional and amateur experimenters in large numbers kept busy trying to improve the process. Some of the proposals made in photographic publications must have startled even the most unorthodox readers. In the mid-1850s, for example, London's *Journal of the Photographic Society* recommended dipping the sensitized plate into pure honey. This procedure, the *Journal* stated, would preserve sensitivity for at least four weeks before exposure, and for 12 hours between exposure and development. The British *Photographic News* prescribed raspberry syrup for the same purpose. Although there is no evidence that any sizable body of photographers followed these suggestions, the concept was not without some merit. Sugary substances, such as honey and syrup, absorbed atmospheric dampness and did help to keep the plates moist and sensitive.

The need for moisture to sustain sensitivity became less important, however, as gradual improvements in formulation of the silver compounds led to faster emulsions. But in the 1880s two separate though related innovations not only made a fast dry plate but also eliminated the need for the clumsy, fragile glass plate itself. The first development was an emulsion based on gelatin—the jelly-like substance that is processed from cattle bones and hides. (Bingham had actually described the process in 1850.) It retained its speed when dry and, perhaps more important, could be applied on a flexible backing—rolls of film—instead of glass. While glass plates coated with gelatin emulsion continued to be used by professional photographers for many decades (astronomers still use them sometimes), roll film revolutionized photography by making it simple enough for millions of amateurs to enjoy.

Most of the credit for bringing photography to the millions goes to one imaginative, hard-driving man, George Eastman, who contributed several of the basic inventions himself, financed research for others and appropriated at least one key development from its originator. A prototype for America's rags-to-riches tradition, he began as an almost penniless bank clerk in Rochester, New York, built one of the country's foremost industrial enterprises, became a millionaire and gave over $100 million away to the arts and education (the University of Rochester and the Eastman School of Music, Tuskegee and Hampton Institutes). Yet he was not a tycoon in the standard mold; he never married, he kept much of his philanthropy anonymous (the several millions he gave to the Massachusetts Institute of Technology were for years credited to a mysterious "Mr. X"), and at the age of 78, after a long illness, he shot himself.

Almost from the day Eastman bought his first camera in 1877, he took a jaundiced view of the wet plate. "I bought an outfit," he said, "and learned that it took not only a strong but also a dauntless man to be an outdoor photographer." Soon he was reading all the photographic literature he could find in search of a less burdensome means of taking pictures. "It seemed," he said, "that one ought to be able to carry less than a pack-horse load." An article in a British publication about a gelatin emulsion that could be used when dry, he said, "started me in the right direction."

Although Eastman knew nothing of chemistry—he had left school when he was 14 to help support his widowed mother—he began to experiment with his own gelatin emulsion. "My first results did not amount to much," he said, "but finally I came upon a coating of gelatin and silver bromide that had all the necessary photographic qualities. . . . At first I wanted to make photography simpler merely for my own convenience, but soon I thought of the possibilities of commercial production." Working at night, often foregoing sleep, he began devising a machine to mass produce dry plates.

By 1880 he had rented space in Rochester, had trained three assistants and had begun selling his plates to various photographic supply houses. He kept his job at the bank, however, until 1881 when he went into partnership with Henry Strong, one of the roomers in his mother's boarding house, and formed the Eastman Dry Plate Company. Each man put up $1,000. But Eastman was aware that photography would never become a popular hobby as long as pictures were taken on awkward glass plates. What was needed was something light, inexpensive and flexible enough to put on rollers—in short, film. His goal became obvious when the firm incorporated in 1884 under the name The Eastman Dry Plate and Film Company.

There was nothing new about the concept of roll film. Almost from Daguerre's time, a number of men had tried with varying degrees of success to make it, but no one was able to produce it commercially until Eastman invented the equipment to manufacture film on a mass basis. The result was Eastman's "American Film," a roll of paper coated with a thin gelatin emulsion. After the film was developed, the emulsion had to be stripped from the opaque paper backing to provide a negative that light could shine through for making prints. Most photographers had trouble with this operation—the negative often stretched when removed from the paper—so the film was usually sent back to the company for processing.

The new film created a great stir among photographers but it had little immediate meaning for the general public since the heavy, expensive view camera was still necessary to take pictures. But roll film made possible a new kind of camera—inexpensive, light and simple to operate—that made everyone a potential photographer. In June 1888 Eastman introduced the Kodak. It came loaded with enough film for 100 pictures. When the roll was used up, the owner merely sent the camera with the exposed film still in it back to the Eastman company in Rochester. Soon the developed and printed photographs and the camera, reloaded with film, were returned to the owner.

The roll-film Kodak became an international sensation almost overnight.

In the midst of all the excitement that followed the introduction of American Film and the Kodak, few people paid any attention to a patent application filed in May 1887 by a New Jersey clergyman named Hannibal Goodwin. Yet Goodwin was the inventor of truly modern roll film: a transparent flexible plastic coated with a thin emulsion and sturdy enough to be used without a paper support (as it is in most modern films).

Goodwin's starting point was a material developed in 1863 from the very substance that had served as the wet plate's emulsion base: collodion. Mixed with camphor, collodion became the versatile plastic, celluloid, which could be rolled, molded and extruded into many different forms and was used for handles on combs and brushes and for gentlemen's detachable collars. But commercially produced celluloid had severe shortcomings for Goodwin's purposes; it was not uniformly transparent and it became brittle after a short time. Goodwin modified celluloid with solvents and finally was able to produce this base at "two one-thousandths of an inch, more or less, in thickness." At first the film tended to curl because the base was coated on only one side. Goodwin eliminated the problem by coating the other side with nonsensitized gelatin.

But Goodwin's patent was not granted until September 1898, more than 11 years after he had made application. The reason for the delay was a condition common to parsons, a lack of funds. Goodwin could not afford to make tests the Patent Office required. Meanwhile, in April 1889 the Eastman Company filed an application for a similar film and was granted it in December of that year. Marketing of the film had begun four months earlier.

By 1900, about two years after his patent had been granted, Goodwin managed to raise enough money to begin manufacturing his film. Before his newly organized firm, the Goodwin Film and Camera Company, could begin operations, however, Goodwin died. Not long after his death, the Goodwin Company filed suit against Eastman for patent infringement, claiming that the Eastman company had departed from its own formula and was using Goodwin's. Litigation dragged on for 12 years before the United States Circuit Court of Appeals finally ruled that Goodwin's patent application of 1887 had "disclosed for the first time the fundamental and essential features of a successful rollable film." By then ownership of the Goodwin patent had changed hands several times and the court award—$5 million—went to the current owners, The Ansco Film Company.

Financial circles may have been interested in the judgment but it meant little to the man on the street. For him the new era in photography had begun with the simple, light camera and roll film. He was too busy snapping pictures to be concerned with who received credit for what. □

Old-Time Processes: Clumsy but Beautiful

In terms of the quality of the picture—in sharpness of the details captured and in the great breadth of the shading reproduced—black-and-white photography was born full bloom when Louis Daguerre introduced the first practical process early in 1839. "A good daguerreotype," says Edward Steichen, one of the modern era's leading photographers, "was as perfect a kind of photograph as was ever made." Daguerreotypes like the portrait of President John Quincy Adams (opposite) represented a major technological triumph, rather as though the first phonograph had been able to reproduce sound as naturally as the finest modern hi-fi set.

Other early processes that followed the daguerreotype were quite remarkable in different ways. The calotype, the first photograph that could be printed from a negative, had its own distinctive look: a soft, rich warmth deriving partly from the fibers of the paper on which the negative was made. A third process—the glass plate coated with a wet collodion emulsion—was capable of a wide range of effects: sharpness approximating that of the daguerreotype, unusual softness in tones of gray and an almost grainless clarity.

The great range of possibilities offered by the old processes, along with a growing interest in the history of photography, has led a number of photographers to experiment with them, difficult as they are to use. Joel Snyder, a Chicago photographer, is one who has turned to the half-forgotten techniques of the 19th Century to achieve results impossible with modern film. Over a period of five years he has tried no less than 15 different processes, using the soft, flattering qualities of the calotype for portraits, and the clear yet faintly old-fashioned appearance of the wet-plate to create advertisements (in one, for a gourmet seasoning, he arranged a still life of food to capture the nostalgic appearance of "chicken like great-grandmother used to make").

Snyder, who demonstrates the three major 19th Century processes on the following pages, has found them fascinating—but highly exacting and, in the case of the daguerreotype and wet plate, dangerous because of the materials employed. One of the old instruction books he has used warns, "Ventilate your mercury—its fume is loaded with rheumatism, sciatica, lumbago, toothache, neuralgia and decrepitude." Mercury can actually, over a long period of time, cause worse harm—partial paralysis—but even temporary effects are very unpleasant, as Snyder has learned: he has suffered severe chest pains and shortness of breath for days after standing too close to fumes from heated mercury. While working with the wet-plate process, he has lost consciousness as a result of inhaling vapors from the ether and alcohol in collodion.

SOUTHWORTH & HAWES: *John Quincy Adams*, c. 1848

1 | The Art of Making a Daguerreotype

1 | **cleaning the plate**

2 | **polishing with a soft cloth**

3 | **preparing iodine crystals for sensitizing**

4 | **sensitizing the plate**

5 | **taking the picture**

NOTE: Because of the hazardous materials involved, readers are warned not to attempt the daguerreotype process shown here, or the wet-plate process (pages 72-73). Even the calotype process (pages 66-67) requires care to avoid silver-nitrate burns.

When Joel Snyder begins to make a daguerreotype, he remembers the advice of the inventor of the process: for good results, the plate of silver-coated copper must be spotlessly clean and highly polished. He soaks a wad of cot-ton in a mixture of pumice and alcohol and thoroughly cleans the surface (1). Next, he buffs the plate to a high gloss (2), using soft lamb's wool.

Now Snyder prepares to sensitize the plate by placing a bowl of iodine crystals (3) at the bottom of an airtight cylinder. With only a candle for illumination—the light level must be low during this stage—Snyder suspends the plate, silver side down, on the two wires inside the top of the cylinder (4). He leaves the plate in place for about 10 minutes, while fumes from the iodine crystals rise to the silver coating on the plate and combine with it to form the light-sensitive compound, silver iodide. To increase sensitivity, Snyder exposes the plate to fumes from a bromine-lime mixture for two minutes, then returns to the iodine for two more minutes. Finally he puts the plate into the camera and poses the model (5), his wife.

After the exposure has been made, Snyder returns to the candlelit dark-room to prepare for developing. This

6 | preparing mercury for developing

7 | the developed image

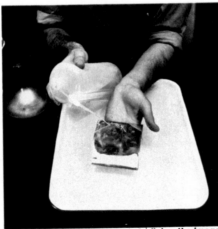

8 | fixing the image

In making the daguerreotype of his wife at right, Joel Snyder used a 4 x 5 Sinar view camera with a plate holder adapted to accept the relatively thick silver-surfaced metal plate. The exposure was 7 seconds at f/4.5.

9 | the finished daguerreotype

process is carried out inside an airtight box to avoid harm from mercury fumes, but in the picture above, the box has been removed to show the steps. Snyder first pours mercury into a bowl supported above a spirit lamp (6). After putting a thermometer in the mercury and lighting the lamp, he quickly lowers it into the box and fastens the top.

He looks through a window in the box and when the thermometer shows that the mercury has reached a temperature of between 140°F. and 180°F., he places the exposed plate in a holder, unseals a slot near the top of the box and inserts the holder so that the silver side of the plate is exposed to the rising mercury fumes. The forming image can be watched by looking through the window of the box—the picture is reflected in the bowl of mercury (7). Finally Snyder pours photographic fixer (sodium thiosulfate) on the plate (8) to make the image permanent. Then he washes the plate in distilled water. The result is a sharply defined daguerreotype (9).

The Several Faces of a Daguerreotype

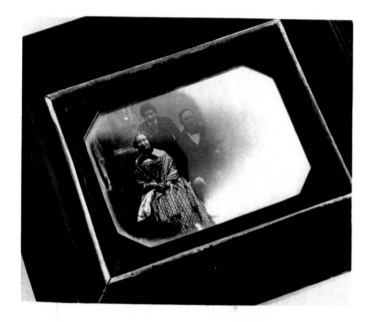

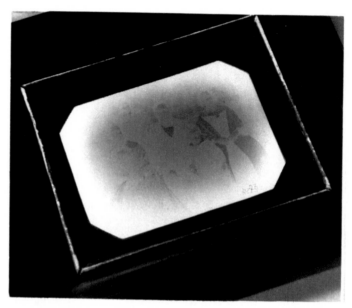

Brilliantly lifelike though the daguerreotype was, it suffered one technical drawback that could not be overcome: when someone looked at the picture, he saw a negative image, a positive image or a combination of the two, depending on his angle of view and the direction of the light striking the photograph. Therefore a daguerreotype, unlike a painting, was not suitable for hanging on a wall.

If, for example, three visitors were looking at this family portrait hanging above the mantelpiece in the parlor, the person on the right side of the room might see the picture as shown above left—half positive and half negative. To the guest standing directly in front of the photograph, it might appear as shown above right—all negative. Only the third person, seated on the left side of the room might see a wholly positive image, as shown opposite.

The simplest way for someone to look at the daguerreotype was to hold it in his hands and shift it slightly until the positive image became visible. This inconvenience, however, seemed insignificant to the thousands of people who thronged newly opened studios in the 1840s to have their portraits made quickly and inexpensively.

PHOTOGRAPHER UNKNOWN: *Family Portrait*, c. 1850

A Clear View of the World in Daguerreotypes

Some people, particularly middle-aged and elderly ones, found the detail in their daguerreotype portraits somewhat distressing; a little less honesty would have been appreciated. But this quality of superb definition made the daguerreotype ideal for recording the wonders of nature and the works of man. The photographs conveyed a sense of reality and immediacy that no artist could match.

Soon after the mechanics of Daguerre's invention were revealed, pho-tographers all over the globe began to take pictures of everything from the Pyramids of Egypt to the busy Cincinnati waterfront *(below)*.

The Cincinnati photograph—actually two photographs carefully fitted together—is an especially good example of the daguerreotype's impressive sharpness—signs on buildings a considerable distance from the water's edge are legible. Even today the picture's fine detail could be matched only by the best modern equipment expertly used.

Niagara Falls (left) was already a world-famous tourist attraction when Platt Babbitt made a daguerreotype of it about 1855. Despite the long exposure required, the visitors in the foreground and the rushing water are recorded with remarkable clarity. In 1848, when Charles Fontayne and William Southgate Porter took their daguerreotypes of the Cincinnati waterfront (below), they used eight plates—two of which are shown here—to encompass the city's entire docking area along the Ohio River.

PLATT D. BABBITT: *Group at Niagara Falls*, c. 1855

WILLIAM SOUTHGATE PORTER AND CHARLES FONTAYNE: *Cincinnati Waterfront*, 1848

2 | Calotype: Prints from a Paper Negative

A calotype is not only somewhat simpler to make than a daguerreotype; the process is also more familiar: the camera produces a negative that can be printed in more or less the normal way.

Joel Snyder carefully selects the paper for the negative—a vellum tracing paper, 100 per cent rag content, free of bleaching agents and mineral impurities and as thin as possible. After washing and drying the paper to remove sizing (which might interfere with absorption of chemicals), he works by candlelight as he sensitizes the sheet,

coating it on one side by floating it for about three minutes on a four per cent solution of silver nitrate in distilled water (1). He lets this coating dry and then floats the paper on a seven per cent potassium iodide solution for one to two minutes; the two chemicals react to form a coating of silver iodide. He then washes the paper in distilled water (2) to remove excess chemicals and again dries the paper.

Now Snyder, still working by candlelight, inspects the paper for imperfections (3). If there are any air bubbles, or

blue or green specks, which indicate mineral deposits in the paper or a residue from the water, he discards the sheet and starts again. If none of these flaws are present, he brushes the paper with a solution of gallic acid, silver nitrate and acetic acid to increase sensitivity (4). The wet paper is now ready for use in the camera.

After the picture is taken (5), he develops the negative by brushing it a second time with the solution of gallic acid, silver nitrate and acetic acid (6). Development may take anywhere from

1 | **coating the paper with silver nitrate**

2 | **washing the paper**

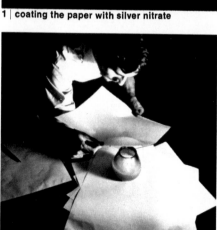

3 | **inspecting for imperfections**

4 | **increasing sensitivity**

5 | **preparing to make the exposure**

one to three minutes depending on how long the paper was exposed in the camera (if the exposure is long enough the image may be visible when the negative comes out of the camera). The negative is then washed, fixed and dried in the normal way. To increase the translucency of the paper for print-making and to minimize the shadows cast by its fibers, Snyder places the negative on a slightly heated surface, such as a cookie sheet, and applies beeswax to one side (7). Now the negative goes into a standard printing frame (8), the blank back of the paper against the glass. A sheet of good bond paper, coated with silver chloride by floating it on a two-and-a-half per cent ammonium chloride solution and a ten per cent solution of silver nitrate, is placed sensitized surface down on top of the negative. In the printing process (9), which takes about 10 minutes, light passes through the glass and paper negative to the printing paper. No developing is necessary —the image is formed directly by the exposure—but fixing and washing are required. Then the print is ready (10).

10 | the finished calotype

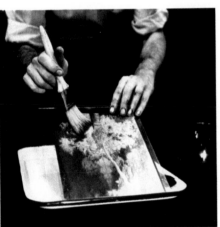

6 | developing the negative

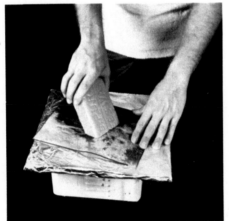

7 | waxing the negative

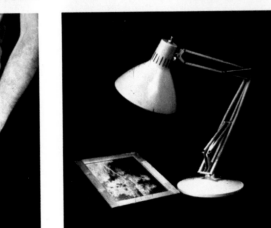

8 | placing the negative in a printing frame

9 | making a contact print

In making a calotype of the wooded scene above—a small inlet in Chicago's Jackson Park—Snyder used his Sinar view camera and an exposure of 2 seconds at f/5.6.

The Soft Look of the Calotype

Because of the texture in both paper negative and printing paper, the calotype process produces a much softer picture than the shiny silver surface of the daguerreotype. Lines lose their distinct edges and details become hazy.

Although most 19th Century photographers preferred the sharply defined daguerreotype, there were many who used the calotype exclusively. Like the unknown photographer who caught a hint of sternness in the portrait shown here (in both negative and positive forms), they found the softness an asset rather than a liability.

The calotype's quality suggests an artist's charcoal drawing and many photographers used it deliberately to create picturesque scenes, particularly of architecture, landscapes and still lifes. The inventor of the process, William Henry Fox Talbot, seemed to share this impression and many of his best pictures are devoted to such subjects.

PHOTOGRAPHER UNKNOWN: *Portrait of a French Lady,* c. 1840

The Inventor's Own Calotypes

To the English country gentleman who invented the calotype, William Henry Fox Talbot, the "hand-sketched" look of the prints probably had considerable personal appeal. It had been his interest in art and the unhappy discovery of his lack of the draftsman's skill that led him to the invention of a photographic process. He became a sensitive, careful photographer with a good sense of composition and made such tasteful calotypes as those shown here.

Although Talbot was the inventor of the negative-positive system of photography now in use, he never received the recognition and financial rewards that Daguerre enjoyed—despite the fact he was only a few days behind Daguerre in publicly announcing his process for recording photographic images.

WILLIAM HENRY FOX TALBOT: *The Chess Players*, c. 1842

WILLIAM HENRY FOX TALBOT (or associate): *The Ruins of Pompeii*, c. 1840

3 | Making a Wet Plate

1 | cleaning the plate

2 | filling the sensitizing bath

3 | coating the plate with collodion

4 | sensitizing the plate

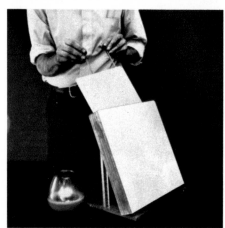

5 | checking the sensitizing

6 | preparing to make the exposure

When Joel Snyder sets out to use the wet-plate process, he starts with a piece of ordinary window glass. To protect his hands from cuts, he sands the edges and a border on the surface of about an eighth of an inch with emery paper. This also improves the bond between the glass and the viscous emulsion that will coat it. Then he washes the glass with a mixture of powdered pumice and alcohol (1).

The next step is to fill a sensitizing bath—a rectangular glass tank—nearly to the top with a solution of one part of silver nitrate to 12 parts of water (2). Now he pours collodion containing potassium iodide on the plate (3) and tilts it back and forth until the entire surface is covered evenly.

Working with only a candle for illumination, he uses glass hooks to lower the collodion-coated plate into the sensitizing bath (4), where he leaves it for four to six minutes. When he pulls the plate out (5), Snyder examines it to see if it is properly sensitized. It should be creamy white. If it looks waxy, more time in the bath is needed. When the plate is ready, Snyder places it, still wet, in a holder and inserts the holder in his camera. Now he is ready to pose his subject (6).

After taking the picture, Snyder returns to the darkroom while the plate is still wet and develops it with pyrogallic acid (7). Then the plate is washed, fixed and washed again. After it has dried, Snyder prints it (8) on paper he sensitizes himself with silver chloride.

7 | developing the plate

To make the collodion wet-plate portrait at right, Snyder posed an actor-director friend in a window, set his view camera at an aperture of f/5.6 and made an exposure of 9 seconds.

8 | the finished portrait

The Wet Plate: De Luxe and Economy Models

Some of the finest portraits in the annals of photography were taken with collodion wet plates. Under studio conditions and in the hands of a skilled photographer, the wet plate could capture mood, the sophisticated interplay of highlights and shadows, textures and details about as well as the finest modern film. Only romantic poses and old-fashioned dress set apart a number of 19th Century photographs, like the one of Sarah Bernhardt at right, from the best of today's portraits.

For actresses, politicians and others in the public eye, the existence of a negative, and thus the means of securing an unlimited number of prints, was important. But there was a large public to whom this advantage was of little interest. The average man was likely to want only a single picture of himself or members of his family to place on the piano or tuck away in a photo album. To meet the demands of this market, the ambrotype *(opposite right)*—from the Greek *ambrotos* for "immortal" and *typos* for "image" —came into being.

This process depended on the wet plate but used it in a special way. Photographers had noticed that when a negative was placed, emulsion side up, against a dark background, a positive image could be seen. This phenomenon was exploited by gluing black cloth to the back of the negative or coating the back with a dark varnish. Copies could no longer be made from the negative, but the elimination of the need for making a print saved money and time. The customer paid less for his photograph—and, by waiting a short time for the backing to be applied, he could take his picture with him.

NADAR: *Sarah Bernhardt, 1859*

PHOTOGRAPHER UNKNOWN: *The Riding Master*, c. 1860

*The ambrotype is simply a collodion wet-plate
negative with a dark backing of either cloth
or varnish. The right half of the plate shown
above is not backed and therefore looks like an
ordinary negative. With backing on the left
side, the positive image appears. A completely
backed plate is shown at right.*

PHOTOGRAPHER UNKNOWN: *Soldier*, c. 1860

The Tintype: A Picture While You Wait

In 1856 soon after the introduction of the economical ambrotype, Hannibal L. Smith, professor of chemistry at Kenyon College, patented the still cheaper, quick-service tintype, which delivered a finished picture even faster than the ambrotype. The fast delivery came from new, rapid processing solutions, the low cost from the tintype's materials. Like the ambrotype, the tintype was a collodion wet-plate negative on a dark background, which resulted in a positive image. But instead of a glass plate backed with dark cloth or varnish, Hannibal used a metal sheet, usually thin iron enameled black or chocolate brown, to support the collodion.

The inexpensive tintypes quickly became the rage of the era. Enterprising tintypists appeared everywhere, taking pictures of children in parks, of families at company picnics, of newly married couples outside churches. Hundreds of thousands of young men, self-conscious in their new uniforms, posed stiffly for the tintype camera before going off to the Civil War. The results were generally crude, but in the hands of a talented photographer the tintype process could produce striking portraits such as the one at right.

Although no copies could be made of tintypes, many photographers used special multi-lensed cameras to take several pictures at once and accommodate anyone who wanted extra photographs of himself. Even after roll film and the simple box camera made every man his own photographer, tintype purveyors prospered. They were fairly common in the United States as late as the 1930s and a number of practitioners are still to be found in South America and other parts of the world. ☐

PHOTOGRAPHER UNKNOWN: *Portrait of an Indian*, c. 1860

PHOTOGRAPHER UNKNOWN: *William Henry Jackson, with his 20 x 24-inch view camera, photographing Zuñi Pueblo near Laguna, New Mexico, c. 1877*

Recording an Era

In May 1842 a gigantic fire swept through Hamburg, Germany, killing 100 persons, destroying more than 4,000 buildings and rendering a fifth of the population homeless. Almost before the embers were cold, two photographers, Carl F. Stelzner and Hermann Biow, were picking their way through the rubble of the gutted city. Loaded down with a heavy camera, silvered plates, dark tent, chemicals and sensitizing and development equipment, they made 40 daguerreotypes of the aftermath of the tragedy *(opposite page)*. Their pictures, taken only three years after the birth of photography, were probably the first news photographs in history.

Stelzner and Biow were among a rapidly growing body of photographers who saw their role as basically that of reporters, conveyors of information about the world and times in which they lived. To them, immediacy and reality were the major strengths of photography, not its ability to render "art" in paintinglike landscapes, still lifes or contrived allegorical tableaux. During the first half century or so after Daguerre had startled the world with his invention, these pioneers blazed the trail of what we now call documentary photography. Their subjects were as varied as the world itself: heads of state juggling the destiny of nations and housewives haggling with street vendors; bloody conflicts and placid scenes in village squares; the ruins of ancient civilizations and the growth of new ones; faraway places and familiar cities. Burdened with their cumbersome paraphernalia, these photographers climbed mountains and descended into mines, went aloft in balloons, crossed deserts, navigated unexplored rivers and risked their lives on battlefields to bring back pictures people wanted to see.

Although there were no means of reproducing these pictures directly in newspapers and magazines until the half-tone mechanical process for making engravings from photographs was developed late in the 19th Century, they enjoyed a surprisingly wide audience. Many people bought prints singly for their private collections. Others acquired books—*Egypt, Sinai and Palestine; Mont Blanc and its Glaciers*—with the photographs painstakingly pasted to the pages. Eventually weekly news journals began copying photographs and printing the results in the form of wood engravings. But the greatest popularity of documentary photographs came in mid-century with the invention of the stereoscopic camera, which made a pair of views that were printed together, side by side, on one card. Looked at through a special viewer, or stereoscope—one of the most popular was designed by the Boston humorist, physician and photography buff, Oliver Wendell Holmes—the two pictures merged to create a scene with three-dimensional depth. The oak-trimmed stereoscope and its stack of 3-D picture cards became a standard adjunct to the Victorian parlor, providing millions of people with a new and exciting concept of their world.

CARL F. STELZNER: *Hamburg,* 1842

Making the world's first news photographs, Carl F. Stelzner took this daguerreotype of the 1842 Hamburg fire from a rooftop near the Elbe River to show the ruins in the Alster district. In the foreground the banks of a canal are strewn with the rubble of buildings, docks and a bridge.

Although portraits and travel photographs were what most people wanted to buy, men like Stelzner and Biow quickly recognized the unique ability of the camera to freeze a moment in time, to record an important happening with such authenticity that anyone looking at the photograph felt almost as though he were witnessing the event. For the first time, through photography, a clerk in London, a mechanic in Boston or a waiter in Paris could be present, at least vicariously, at such historic occasions as the coronation of King Wilhelm of Prussia, the great gathering assembled on St. Peter's Square to hear Pope Pius IX proclaim the doctrine of papal infallibility or the signing of a peace treaty in China by mandarins and British representatives.

Such early news photography probably had its greatest public impact in the reporting of war. When the United States and Mexico fought in the late 1840s, photographers were on hand to take pictures of the troops on both sides. At about the same time, a photographer recorded a Russian army of occupation that had come to help the Austro-Hungarian Empire control rebellious Hungarians. But these ventures produced only a few stilted pictures of soldiers in formation. Modern reportage of war was born and matured in the decade between 1855 and 1865, the years when photographers went to the battlefields of the Crimean War and the United States Civil War. The ways in which the two conflicts were documented differ enormously, as can be seen in the work of the photographer most closely connected with each war: Roger Fenton, who was with the British, French and Turkish forces in the Crimea, and Mathew Brady, who headed the photographic teams that accompanied the Union armies fighting the Confederacy.

Fenton's war was fought in the hills and valleys of the Crimean borderland between Russia and Turkey. Russian expansionist pressures had led Turkey to declare war in October 1853; the following March England and France became allies of the Turks. Shortly before England entered the conflict, a British publication, *The Practical Mechanics' Journal,* proposed that photography be used "to obtain undeniably accurate representations of the realities of war and its contingent scenery, its struggles, its failures and its triumphs." Combat artists had illustrated battle scenes before, but the work of the painter, the *Journal* said, "is powerless in attempting to describe what occurs in such operations, whilst a photographic picture brings the thing itself before us." In its enthusiasm for the essential "truth" of photography, the *Journal* overlooked the fact that the photographer chooses which "truths" will be his subjects.

England had been at war for about a year when Roger Fenton, a 35-year-old lawyer and amateur artist-photographer, was personally selected by Queen Victoria and Prince Albert to go to the Crimea (the venture was financed by the Manchester publishing house of Thomas Agnew & Sons).

The royal couple had little, if any, interest in Fenton's photographing "the realities of war" and certainly none in his recording "its failures." On the contrary, he may have received explicit instructions to avoid that sort of thing; the home-front populace was already getting too much of it from newspaper reporters on the scene.

During the autumn of 1854 and the winter that followed, the British press was filled with stories about the dreadful conditions under which the troops lived and the almost criminal maladministration of the war. William Howard Russell of *The Times* of London was especially vehement. In late November he wrote that the men were in the midst of a winter campaign without warm, waterproof clothing and that "not a soul seems to care for their comfort, or even for their lives." In a December dispatch he wrote: "The dead, laid out as they died, are lying side by side with the living. . . . The commonest accessories of a hospital are wanting . . . for all I can observe, these men die without the least effort being made to save them." Casualty lists bore out such grisly accounts. Of the men who died in the Crimea, seven eighths were victims of cholera and exposure; only one eighth died in battle. Just before Fenton was to leave for the war in early February 1855, popular outrage forced the resignation of the incumbent prime minister, Lord Aberdeen. In this highly volatile political situation, the Queen almost surely ordered Fenton to take no pictures that would further arouse the anger of the citizens.

Fenton and his two assistants arrived at Balaclava in the Crimea on March 8, 1855. With them they brought a van that had been converted into a combination darkroom and living quarters, and 36 large cases containing five cameras, a number of lenses of different focal lengths, some 700 unsensitized glass plates, chemicals, a still for purifying water, printing frames, a stove, food, wine, harnesses for four horses and a set of carpenter's tools. Fenton would be using the relatively new wet plates, which had to be prepared immediately before use but permitted considerably shorter exposures than earlier materials.

In Balaclava, Fenton was shocked by the indifference to even elementary sanitation. "The whole place is one great pigsty," he wrote. "At present eighty sheep are slaughtered every day in the vessels in harbour alone, and the entrails thrown into the water alongside. All over the camp, animals wanted for food are killed close to the tents, and the parts not used are rotting for days." However, such scenes, which would have offended Victorian tastes as well as Victoria herself, were not subjects for Fenton's camera.

In contrast to the soldiers, Fenton lived fairly well during the months he was in the Crimea. He was welcomed into the top military circles, where good food, vintage wines and other amenities were routine. But in his work he shared the danger and hardship of the front. His van, painted a light color

ROGER FENTON: *Field Kitchen of the 8th Hussars, the Crimea,* 1855

The war in the Crimea appeared comfortable enough in Roger Fenton's pictures of nattily uniformed soldiers being served a meal in the field and the neat encampment of an artillery unit (opposite). What they failed to record was the other face of the conflict: men in inadequate clothing shivering in the cold and rain, abominable sanitary conditions that led to cholera epidemics—and the theatrical military bumbling, pain and wholesale death that marked this "last of the gentlemen's wars."

ROGER FENTON: *Encampment of Horse Artillery, the Crimea,* 1855

to reflect heat, could be seen for miles on the battlefield; it frequently became the target of Russian artillerymen, who probably thought it was an ammunition wagon. On one occasion, a shell tore off its roof. Fortunately Fenton and his assistants were not injured. A far worse trial for the photographer and his helpers was the intense, dry heat of early summer and the accompanying dust and swarms of flies. The van became an oven that cooked the men and their materials. "When my van door is closed before the plate is prepared," Fenton wrote, "perspiration is running down my face, and dropping like tears. . . . The developing water is so hot I can hardly bear my hands in it." All the darkroom work became extremely difficult. Cleaning plates became a major problem. Minute foreign substances on the glass, which created no difficulties in more moderate temperatures, now reacted chemically to the heat and caused spots and streaks on the negative. Coating large plates with their emulsion was a maddening task. Even though the collodion was thinned, it often dried where it was first poured before the edges were covered. And when a plate was properly prepared, the collodion would frequently dry—drastically reducing its sensitivity—within the few minutes required to insert the plate in a frame, get it to the camera, take the picture and return to the darkroom for development.

Despite such handicaps, Fenton took many excellent pictures *(pages 82-83)*. He was unable to capture action because of the relatively long exposure required even by wet plates, but his photographs of officers and men look remarkably spontaneous and unposed. They reveal, however, a highly selective view of war—a war without death or destruction, without horror or suffering or fear. We see an officer about to enjoy a glass of wine after a hard day in the field, a group of soldiers teaching a dog to sit up, gunners taking a siesta near a mortar. Only a few pictures, such as "The Tombs of Cathcarts Hill" (a half dozen or so headstones and men raising a flag) and "The Valley of the Shadow of Death" (a deserted road strewn with cannonballs) offer even a slight reminder that war is a lethal business.

Although men who had served in the Crimea may have had reservations about Fenton's one-sided portrayal of the war, Queen Victoria, her government and the British public apparently had none. When Fenton returned to England in July 1855, he was warmly received by the royal family and arrangements were immediately made to exhibit his several hundred pictures in London and other English cities. Portfolios of prints were published and single pictures were also put on the market. In terms of counteracting, at least partially, the effects of the grim reporting and casualty lists from the Crimea, Fenton's mission was a success.

In the early summer of 1861, just six years after Fenton had returned to London, President Abraham Lincoln, deeply immersed in plans for the first major battles of the Civil War, took time to listen to the request of a photographer and then to scribble a two-word note: "Pass Brady." By granting the famous portrait photographer, Mathew Brady, permission to travel anywhere with the Union armies, Lincoln cleared the way for a kind of photographic recording of war never seen before *(pages 96-103)*.

Pictures of wars and other news events brought the realities of life home to millions for the first time. But once over, such realities were soon forgotten; Brady, for one, could hardly sell a war picture after the conflict came to an end. People were far more fascinated with photographs of the exotic won-

TIMOTHY H. O'SULLIVAN: *The Photographer's Wagon and Mules in the Nevada Desert,* 1868

*To capture the lonely vastness of the desert north
of Death Valley, Timothy H. O'Sullivan climbed a
sand dune and made this picture of the
ambulance that served as his photographic van.*

ders of the world. True, there had always been artists' drawings that portrayed unfamiliar places. But looking at drawings meant seeing things through another person's eyes and never quite believing them. The camera somehow seemed an extension of one's own vision; a photograph was accepted as real, a faithful image created by a mechanical process.

Through photography, the stay-at-home of the 19th Century could travel by proxy to almost any part of the world. Some of the finest photographers of the era served as his guides. In 1856 Francis Frith, a British photographer and publisher, struggled 600 miles up the Nile to the Second Cataract, bringing back pictures of the Pyramids, the Sphinx and ancient temples along the route *(pages 110-111)*. The Bisson brothers, Louis Auguste and Auguste Rosalie, hauled their equipment to altitudes of 16,000 feet in the French Alps to photograph the peaks, while Carlo Ponti and James Anderson portrayed the watery wonders of Venice and the ruins of ancient Rome.

Strangely enough, one of the most spectacular landscapes of all, on the western frontier of the United States, remained largely unphotographed until the decade following the end of the Civil War. Explorers and artists had been in the Rocky Mountain area long before this time, but the wondrous tales they had told of the region and the sketches they had made were often discounted. Most of these doubts were dispelled when photographers made the western trek. One of the first to go was Timothy H. O'Sullivan, who had worked with Brady before and during the Civil War *(page 98)*.

The hardships and dangers of the Civil War—on two occasions O'Sullivan's camera was toppled by shell fragments while he was taking pictures —proved excellent schooling for his work with government surveying teams in the West. On his first expedition to the Rockies in 1867, the party faced passes blocked with snow drifts of 30 feet or more, capable of swallowing men and mules without a trace. To lessen the hazard, the group moved at night when the bitter cold froze the snow into somewhat firmer footing. One night, O'Sullivan later recounted, 13 grueling hours were required to cross a two-and-a-half mile divide. Hauling mules out of holes in the snow consumed much of the time.

On that same trip, the rapids of the Truckee River in what is now Nevada almost cost O'Sullivan his life. Fortunately he escaped with only a financial loss. The small boat in which he and several other men were traveling was driven off course by the swift current and wedged between two rocks. The men tried to shove off with their oars and succeeded only in losing them. Stripping to his underwear, the photographer dived into the stream to free the boat and was immediately swept under the swirling water. He finally surfaced some distance downstream, managed to swim ashore and yelled to his companions to throw him a line. They did—weighting the end with O'Sul-

3083. CATHEDRAL SPIRES. W.H.J.C°

WILLIAM HENRY JACKSON: *Cathedral Spires in the Garden of the Gods, Colorado, 1873*

Views of the American West, like this one of the spectacularly eroded sandstone pinnacles in the foothills of the Rockies, drew streams of tourists when they were seen back East.

livan's purse containing $300 in $20 gold pieces. The line reached O'Sullivan but not the purse, which fell off and disappeared into the water. "I prospected a long time, barefooted, for it," he sadly reported later.

Photographically, O'Sullivan's trip was more successful. He photographed part of the California desert on that first expedition and expressed his fascination with its brilliant mounds of snow-like sand in both pictures *(pages 84-85)* and words. "The contour of the mounds was undulating and graceful," he recalled, "it being continually broken into the sharp edges by the falling away of some of the portions of the mound, which had been undermined by the keen winds that spring up during the last hours of daylight and continue through the night."

O'Sullivan went on five expeditions to the West and brought back some of the finest pictures ever taken of the region. His work, however, attracted little public attention at the time, and when he died, at age 42 of tuberculosis, he was buried in an unmarked grave on Staten Island in New York.

But not all the early photographers who went west were unappreciated. Probably the most celebrated was William Henry Jackson. Born in Keeseville, New York, in 1843, Jackson had become familiar with cameras during his boyhood, thanks to a father who experimented with daguerreotypes. Young Jackson's first interest was painting and at age 15 he left school to earn his living by painting portraits and landscapes and by hand-coloring photographs. Later he went to Vermont and took a steady job as a photographer's assistant. When the Civil War began, he volunteered for the Union Army, served out his enlistment without seeing combat and then returned to Vermont and photography. He was doing well financially but an unhappy love affair caused him to leave in 1866 and he was soon working his way toward the West Coast, part of the time as a "bullwhacker," or driver, with a wagon train. He finally ended up in Omaha running a photographic studio.

Jackson soon became bored with routine studio work, so he fitted out a wagon as a photographic van and set off to take pictures of Indians. It was not an undertaking for a nervous man. The Union Pacific and Central Pacific were then laying tracks westward for the first transcontinental railroad and the Indians around Omaha were forcibly resisting the technological invasion. There were a number of attacks on work crews. But on his first trip, a six-day excursion from Omaha to Cheyenne and back, Jackson managed to persuade local tribesmen not only to leave his scalp in place but to pose for his cameras. The prints sold readily. Encouraged by his success, he took longer journeys and returned with pictures of such sights as the Salt Lake Valley, the Wasatch Mountains and Echo and Weber canyons.

In the summer of 1870, Jackson accompanied Dr. Ferdinand V. Hayden, a geologist and physician, on a United States government survey along the Oregon Trail through Wyoming. This relationship with Hayden was to lead to Jackson's most significant work a year later: pictures that would play a crucial role in preserving for future generations the beauty of the western wilderness. Hayden, fascinated by what he heard in a lecture about the marvels of Yellowstone, persuaded Congress to underwrite an expedition there in 1871; as soon as he had an appropriation to pay a photographer, he recruited Jackson to join the party.

The expedition left Ogden, Utah, in early June. Most of Jackson's photographic gear was transported in a converted ambulance that also served as a darkroom. When Jackson was working in mountainous areas where the wagon could not go, a sturdy mule called "Hypo" assumed the burden and a specially fitted tent became the darkroom. "When hard pressed for time," Jackson reported later, "I had to make a negative in fifteen minutes from the time the first rope was thrown from the pack to the final repacking."

Photographing Yellowstone was a difficult and often risky business, but Jackson was caught up in the excitement of seeing the area for the first time and being the first to record its wonders with a camera. His earlier photographic experience in the wilderness served him well. He was especially adept at what army men refer to as "field expedients," making do with whatever is at hand. When he photographed Mammoth Hot Springs, for example, he employed the subject itself in his photographic processing. After taking and developing his pictures, he used the 120° water that tumbled down the series of semicircular basins to wash the plates, knowing they would dry more quickly because of the heat of the water.

Fortunately, Jackson was a strong man as well as a resourceful one. Once, after taking a number of pictures at the top of Yellowstone's 200-foot Tower Falls, he decided to take some from the bottom without moving all his heavy equipment. He carried only his camera and a few plates, exposed them, climbed back to the summit, developed them, prepared more plates and went down again. To keep the prepared plates moist and sensitive during the ascent and descent, Jackson backed them with wet blotting paper, inserted them in holders, wrapped the holders in a wet towel and then covered the entire package with a black cloth. The first climb down to the bottom and the last up were the most difficult because he had to carry the camera as well as the plates, but the intervening round trips were not easy; four per day was the maximum possible. Even Jackson admitted he paid "a stiff price in labor for one subject."

The results Jackson achieved were worth the effort. He made about 400 negatives of some of the most magnificent scenery on earth. Great canyons, waterfalls, geysers shooting towers of boiling water into the air, placid lakes, lush forests and forbidding sulphur flats—all were part of his photographic

Three Shoshone squaws and a well-wrapped papoose pose for William Henry Jackson's camera inside the entrance to a tepee. In his travels in the West, Jackson took hundreds of such pictures—of Indian tepee villages and pueblos, of men doing tribal dances and women grinding corn, of proud chiefs sitting for their portraits in full-feathered dress. The photographs constitute one of the few authentic records of the American Indians as they lived before they were confined to reservations.

WILLIAM HENRY JACKSON: *Shoshone Tepee*, c. 1870

report. Many of the earlier explorers had been labeled as liars because of the stories they brought back about Yellowstone; Jackson and his cameras provided incontrovertible evidence that the descriptions had been accurate.

Early in the 1871-1872 session in Congress, Senator S. C. Pomeroy of Kansas had introduced a bill calling for the establishment of America's first national park at Yellowstone. Because of the Senate's reluctance to accept the verbal accounts of the area, he had had considerable difficulty in getting consideration of the measure. But the atmosphere changed completely on the day Pomeroy could say to his colleagues, "There are photographs of the valley and of the curiosities, which the senators can see." Once they had seen Jackson's pictures, the Senate and then the House quickly passed the bill and, on March 1, 1872, President Ulysses S. Grant signed it into law. Yellowstone was now set apart "for the benefit and enjoyment of the public." Jackson's photographs, especially his stereoscopic slides, which were sold in great quantities, also helped start Yellowstone's first tourist boom. Wealthy sportsmen, adventurers and even proper Eastern ladies and their families journeyed to the West to see at first hand the sights Jackson had captured with his camera.

During the next six years, Jackson accompanied Hayden on other expeditions, photographing the Grand Tetons in Wyoming, the Rocky Mountains in the Pike's Peak area and the ruins of the pre-Columbian cliff dwellings of the Mesa Verde in Colorado's San Juan mountains. (In 1906 Mesa Verde also became a national park.) After Jackson's job with the United States Geological Survey was eliminated in an economy move in 1878, he struck out on his own and made a modest fortune photographing various parts of the United States, Canada and Mexico. When the halftone printing process came into use in the 1880s he went into the business of engraving photographs for reproduction in newspapers and magazines; once again he prospered. In 1924, at 81, he moved to Washington, D.C., and resumed his career as a painter, which he had never fully given up. When he was 93, he painted a series of oils of the Old West that still hangs in the museum af the Department of the Interior. He maintained his interest in photography until his death in 1942, just months before he would have celebrated his 100th birthday. His name is not likely to be forgotten. Jackson's Canyon along the Oregon-Mormon Trail on the North Platte River, Jackson's Lake in the Grand Teton Mountains and Jackson's Butte in the Mesa Verde are permanent memorials to a great photographer and his work.

In the same decades in which the camera was documenting the events and places of the world, it was also recording the lives of the people of the world. A number of 19th Century photographers made pictures of influential per-

GIUSEPPE PRIMOLI: *A Reception at the Quirinal Palace,* 1893

GIUSEPPE PRIMOLI: *Attendants at the Wedding of Vittorio Emanuele III*, 1896

As a member of the European aristocracy, Count Giuseppe Napoleone Primoli had ready access to stylish events. One was the silver wedding anniversary of King Umberto I and Queen Margherita at the King's palace in Rome in 1893, whose grand sweep he captured in the photograph opposite. Another was the wedding of King Vittorio Emanuele III to Princess Helena of Montenegro in 1896, whose fringe details he recorded in the picture above.

sonages that were not portraits intended for private use but were meant to be sold to the public. In 1850 Mathew Brady published *The Gallery of Illustrious Americans,* "containing portraits of twelve of the most eminent citizens of the American Republic since the days of Washington. . . ." The citizens then so eminent included Henry Clay, John James Audubon and Daniel Webster as well as the now half-forgotten President, Millard Fillmore, and midwestern politician Lewis Cass. Brady also photographed all but one of the 20 men who had held the office of President of the United States in the years between 1825 and 1897. (The exception was William Henry Harrison, who died in 1841, before Brady became a practicing photographer.)

Late in the century, Giuseppe Primoli, an Italian count and intimate of the aristocracy of France and Italy, provided an extensive photographic record of the rarefied world of European nobility. His pictures of the upper classes at work and play constitute one of the best single portrayals of the period known as *la Belle Époque (pages 90-93).* Primoli, an extraordinarily energetic man, traveled from one end of Europe to the other, recording its sovereigns attending receptions, riding horseback and in carriages, participating in hunting expeditions and military exercises. He was often followed by a small caravan of servants to help him haul around his collection of cameras, his darkroom equipment and his hundreds of glass plates. Like a modern photojournalist, he was not content until he had exhausted a subject, taking many pictures from different angles, documenting all the details of an event. (It is hardly surprising that in his first three years as a photographer he exposed some 10,000 plates.) And, like a modern reporter, he often sought to reveal a situation not by showing the action itself but by recording people's reactions to it; when he went to a local racetrack, for example, he turned his back on the horses and caught instead the richly changing expressions of the spectators in the stands. Anything and everything interested Primoli. When Buffalo Bill and his road company came to Rome, Primoli was right there, pitching his photographic tent next to those of the Indians and persuading them to allow their pictures to be taken. Yet, enthusiastic as he was about photography, Primoli was no dilettante. He was acutely aware of the realities of life; among his best pictures are photographs that show policemen at work, a woman fixing her hair *(pages 92-93),* even beggars and children sleeping in the streets and prisoners in chains.

Perhaps the most penetrating photographic study of urban life, however, was undertaken by John Thomson in London. He focused on the slums of the British capital and became the first photographer to use pictures deliberately for pointed social comment. His reputation as a photographer was established well before he made London's poor his personal cause. Born in Scotland in 1837, he attended the University of Edinburgh and majored in chemistry, but photography soon became his primary interest. In 1862 he boarded a steamer with his cameras and wet-plate equipment and headed for the Far East. His travels to Siam, Cambodia, Formosa, the Malay Peninsula and China—and his revealing photographs of the peoples, cities and landscapes of those countries—became the basis of a four-volume work, written by Thomson and illustrated with lithographs, of a special type called collotypes, made from his photographs. The books made Thomson one of the best-known photographers in Great Britain.

In the 1870s Thomson met a journalist named Adolphe Smith, who suggested that they collaborate on a book about the London slums. Thomson and Smith were soon at work with camera and notebook. The result was *Street Life in London,* consisting of 36 case histories, each of them illustrated with a Thomson photograph reproduced by a method similar to collotype. The book was published in 1877 and, given its subject matter, the timing could not have been better.

Britain was going through a period of extensive self-examination and social change, a period when, in the words of biographer and critic Lytton Strachey, "Victoria found herself condemned to live in an agitating atmosphere of interminable reform. . . ." One of the troublesome questions being asked has a familiar ring today: Why are so many citizens of a progressive and wealthy society forced to live in abject poverty?

Apparently aware that earlier, nonphotographic treatises on the slums had sometimes been dismissed as hyperbole, Thomson and Smith pointed out in their introduction that they were "bringing to bear the precision of photography in illustration of our subject. The unquestionable accuracy of this testimony will enable us to present true types of the London Poor and shield us from the accusation of either underrating or exaggerating individual peculiarities of appearance."

Thomson did achieve a remarkable balance with his photographs *(pages 94-95).* The filth, the ragged clothes, the dismal surroundings, the degradation and despair are all there, but he also shows that warmth, humor and spirit can continue to flourish even under the worst of conditions. A picture like "The Crawlers"—one of a number of middle-aged women who can barely drag themselves from one place to another—is in itself a photographic essay on the indifference of society. The text comments: "Huddled together on the workhouse steps in Shorts Gardens, these wrecks of humanity, the Crawlers of St. Giles, may be seen both day and night seeking mutual warmth and mutual consolation in their extreme misery. As a rule, they are old women reduced by vice and poverty to that degree of wretchedness which destroys even the energy to beg." The same atmosphere of defeat is also present in other photographs such as "London Nomads," in which two

GIUSEPPE PRIMOLI: *Rome Commissioner of Public Safety and Carabinieri, c. 1884*

GIUSEPPE PRIMOLI: *Girl Fixing Her Hair, c. 1895*

Like all gifted reporters, Giuseppe Primoli took pains to catch the small, human moments that occur in the lives of ordinary people, such as the policemen at left, posing with their boss amidst barricades set up for a carnival horse race in the streets of Rome, and the girl above, standing on a stool to primp in a mirror while a very attentive admirer looks on.

A London "Boardman"

Used Furniture Dealer

"Cast Iron Billy" (left), an Omnibus Driver

men and two women, dirty, tired and seemingly devoid of interest in anything, are shown outside a battered, gypsy-like wagon, while two children with already aging faces peer out from the wagon's door.

In contrast to such scenes are others of grinning youngsters buying ices from a man with a pushcart, a family posing self-consciously in a park for a street photographer, a young Italian street musician playing a harp for a small but attentive audience. Many of the photographs simply show the day-to-day activities and haunts of the slum dwellers: a second-hand dress shop in which soiled garments hang as limply as sails on an airless sea; a sidewalk "doctor" selling a "cough preventative"; a locksmith working in his street stall; a shoeshine boy; a water cart flushing the streets; a woman buying strawberries from a vendor; boys looking hungrily through the window of a dingy restaurant while the owner stands in the doorway.

In *Street Life in London,* Thomson was doing with his camera what Charles Dickens had done earlier with a number of his novels: assaulting the British conscience with the hope of improving the lot of the poor. The use of photography as an editorial weapon became more and more common in the decades that followed as photographers lashed out at shameful conditions either ignored or treated with apathy by society. In the 1890s, Jacob A. Riis focused on the slums of New York and produced his memorable book of text and pictures, *How the Other Half Lives,* a damning commentary on indifference to poverty in one of the world's richest cities. A decade later, Lewis W. Hine, employing what he called "photo-interpretations," expressed his indignation over the heartless exploitation of child labor in sweatshop factories; his report was a major factor in the passage of child-labor laws in the United States. During the depression of the 1930s, LIFE and FORTUNE photographer Margaret Bourke-White and novelist Erskine Caldwell collaborated on the powerful *You Have Seen Their Faces,* a photographic essay on the bitter human suffering in the South. Today this tradition of photographic reportage and commentary has become an integral part of modern communications and a major force behind communal action, from the newspaper story on alienated youth to the magazine picture essay on environmental pollution. □

The first known use of photography as a tool of social commentary was a book called "Street Life in London," published in 1877, a collection of essays, as the preface put it, on the "various means by which our unfortunate fellow-creatures endeavour to earn, beg or steal their daily bread." The photographs, some of which are shown here, were taken by John Thomson, who had established a reputation with perceptive portraits as well as with several books of photographs recording Far Eastern cultures. "Street Life" was sold on London newsstands in 12 installments of three photographs and essays each, and added to the growing awareness of urban poverty.

Three Men in a Pub

Shoeshine Boy

"Caney the Clown," Recaning a Chair

Flower Sellers at Covent Garden

London Nomads

A Patent-Medicine Man

One of the "Crawlers," Minding a Child

Bargemen on the Thames

Chimney Sweep

A Famous Chronicle of War

When the Civil War split America, hundreds of men took cameras to the battlefields and brought back a record that, with the honesty only photography can achieve, revealed the tragic truth of combat to people at home. But today it is the name of one man, Mathew Brady, that is almost synonymous with Civil War photography. Even the newspapers of the time had to struggle to find words adequate to their admiration of his work. The *New York World* wrote that Brady and his assistants "have hung on the skirts of every battle scene; have caught the compassion of the hospital, the romance of the bivouac, the pomp and panoply of the field-review—aye, even the cloud of conflict, the flash of the battery, the after-wreck and anguish of the hard won field."

Brady, in fact, may not have taken a single picture of the war. Many pictures attributed to him actually were taken by aides, and notable photographs were made independently by such men as Alexander Gardner, who took the picture on page 100 after leaving Brady's employ.

In another sense, however, Brady deserves full credit for the 7,000 Civil War photographs marketed under his name. A large and efficient corps of photographers was needed to cover the full sweep of the conflict and Mathew Brady was perhaps the only man who could have organized it. As the leading American portrait photographer of his time, he was acquainted with many generals and statesmen—including President Lincoln—and could count on their cooperation.

To cover the war, he dispatched as many as 22 horse-drawn photography wagons to every front—making assignments "like a large newspaper," he later recalled. Each wagon had a light-proof door leading to a boxed-in well that extended below floor level. "The work of coating or sensitizing the plates and that of developing them was done from this well, in which there was just room enough to work," wrote one photographer. "As the operator stood there the collodion was within reach of his right hand, in a special receptacle. On his left also was the holder of one of the baths. The chief developing bath was in front, with the tanks of various liquids stored in front of it, and the space between it and the floor filled with plates. . . . Brady risked his life many a time in order not to separate from this cumbrous piece of impedimenta."

Although Brady spent a good deal of his time running the operation from Washington, he often ventured into the field. On the opposite page he is shown posing *(far right)* at the encampment of one of the Union Army's generals. He looked somewhat out of place with his broad-brimmed felt hat, which, as one reporter said, resembled "that of a Paris art student."

The pictures that Brady's men took were seen far and wide. But, despite their impact as documents of the war, their actual sales were not nearly sufficient to cover the expenses of Brady's small army of photographers. Although he could see himself sinking into bankruptcy as the war dragged on and on, he persisted right to the end—and even persuaded the defeated Confederate leader, General Robert E. Lee, to pose for one of his assistants after the surrender at Appomattox.

Mathew Brady (right), photographed by an assistant while posing with General Robert B. Potter and his staff, c. 1863

A Famous Chronicle of War: continued

Pomp and Boredom in Camp

TIMOTHY H. O'SULLIVAN: *Headquarters Guard (114th Zouaves), Army of the Potomac, Culpeper, Virginia*, c. 1863

Because the six- to ten-second exposure required by the wet-plate process would have blurred moving objects, Civil War photographers usually limited their pictures to lulls in the action. But they turned this handicap to their advantage by capturing the look and feel of Union army camps—the lineups of lads on battlefields far from their homes and the long, dull days of men standing around, passing the time as they waited for orders. Camp life often had a sense of glory as well as tedium. The company shown above, one of several exotically uniformed groups called Zouaves, wore white turbans, blue jackets and scarlet pants. They insisted on retaining their dazzling attire throughout the war, despite the proven dangers of its brilliant visibility.

PHOTOGRAPHER UNKNOWN: *Camp of the Oneida Cavalry Headquarters, Army of the Potomac,* 1865

The Grim Truths of Combat

ALEXANDER GARDNER: *First Pennsylvania Light Artillery, Battery B, Petersburg, Virginia,* 1864

The Civil War photographers often went to the front lines to catch the impressive preparations for battle—and its grisly aftermath. Making such pictures as the one above was dangerous, even if the shooting had not yet begun. Once when Brady himself was supervising a picture of gunners at their cannons, a Confederate lookout spotted the activity and ordered a barrage. Brady calmly continued to work as the earth erupted all around him. During a similar bombardment, another photographer set up his camera in a crater that a shell had just made. When an officer expressed amazement, the man grinned and said, "Two shots never fell in the same place, Cap'n."

Brady's photographers brought back a number of pictures of less fortunate men, such as the felled infantryman *(opposite)* lying beside a spiked device designed to keep the enemy from the trenches. Such pictures were widely circulated and their effect was stunning. After viewing some of the battlefield scenes, one commentator said simply, "Brady never misrepresents."

MATHEW BRADY (or assistant): *Dead Confederate Soldier, Petersburg, Virginia*, 1865

The Aftermath of Battle

Death and destruction were frequent themes of Civil War photographs, even though the pictures that sold best were those that were easier to swallow—heroic generals posing with their troops or formations of the boys from home, still standing tall and straight with their rifles glinting in the sun. As the Union armies swept into the South, photographers were on hand to catch the images of ruin, such as Alexander Gardner's view at right of a burned-out flour mill in Richmond. The sight of the terrible ravages of war saddened the North and South alike. When author-physician (and amateur photographer) Oliver Wendell Holmes saw some Brady photographs of a Civil War battlefield, he wrote, "The sight of these pictures is a commentary on civilization such as the savage might well triumph to show its missionaries." □

ALEXANDER GARDNER: *Ruins of the Gallego Flour Mill, Richmond, Virginia,* 1865

103

The Grand Tour in Pictures

In the 19th Century, travel to foreign lands was too expensive for all but the very rich. Stay-at-homes could learn of the world through books and drawings, but photography added a tempting new dimension by presenting "reality." Enterprising publishers, quick to realize that there was a hungry market for travel photography, soon had camera-wielding emissaries taking pictures of the well-known European cities and even of such exotic wonders as the Kremlin in Moscow *(right)*.

Armchair travelers bought the pictures by the millions, pasting prints in books and projecting glass slides for "magic lantern" shows in schools, churches and lecture halls. But the most popular form of the travel view was the stereoscopic picture, its three-dimensional realism a marvel of Victorian technology. By the 1870s, stores in practically every city in America sold paired pictures, mounted on heavy cardboard and often tinted a rich sepia. Many of the pictures were sold in sets, providing the purchaser with a complete pictorial tour of a city like Paris or a whole country like Scotland or Palestine. Publishers issued catalogues of the views and advertised in local newspapers. "For the Holidays," read a typical blurb from one large publishing house, "we have just received a new and most exquisite Assortment, the cream of the London and Paris markets." Simply by placing an order through the mail an ordinary citizen could see the high spots of civilization —without budging from his home.

ROGER FENTON: *Domes of the Cathedral of the Resurrection, the Kremlin, Moscow, 1852*

Romantic Vistas from Far Away

To capture this serene view of the Swiss city of Interlaken in the Alps, Adolphe Braun, one of the early masters of travel photography, used a special panoramic camera that took in a wide angle of the scene from a nearby hillside. This was one of the easier assignments of his picture-making expedition. It was taxing enough to carry a large camera, chemicals, a tent for developing and other appurtenances over even mildly rough terrain, but Switzerland was another story altogether. To take pictures from one mountain in the Alps, Braun needed the help of 15 porters and guides. He spent three days on the mountain and exposed a total of five plates. The armchair traveler, on the other hand, could enjoy one of Braun's hard-won views for a quarter.

ADOLPHE BRAUN: *Interlaken*, c. 1868

107

Views of Worlds Left Behind

PHOTOGRAPHER UNKNOWN: *View of Rome from the Monte Pincio,* c. 1862

The Roman Empire may have declined and fallen more than a thousand years earlier, but to the 19th Century traveler—armchair variety included—Rome was the one place that had to be seen. Photographs of the city tended to focus on the architectural glories of the past. The sight of the Coliseum stirred strong memories of Christians and lions; the Forum summoned up the spectacle of toga-clad senators ruling the world.

Greece and the Holy Land shared with Rome a special place in the hearts of travelers (would-be and actual), because they too were rich and ancient sources of culture. And to Americans, who were still fashioning a nation out of the savages' wilderness, even a view of the solid houses of the burghers of Hamburg *(opposite)* was a reminder of the traditions on which they hoped to build civilization in the New World.

G. KOPPMAN & CO.: *Houses on a Canal, Hamburg, Germany, 1884*

Wondrous Journeys up the Nile

For many 19th Century travelers Egypt was a principal attraction of the Grand Tour, if only so that they could refer smugly to the fact that they had seen Cairo, the Pyramids and the Sphinx. But few had glimpsed the wonders farther up the Nile before Francis Frith recorded them on wet plates and brought the pictures back to England.

To make his photographs of life on the mighty river *(right)* and of the magnificent temples that lined its banks, Frith traveled in a photographic van he had fitted out to serve as both darkroom and sleeping quarters, its roof shaded from the blazing sun by a loose cover of white sailcloth. This "most conspicuous and mysterious looking vehicle," he later wrote, "excited among the Egyptian populace a vast amount of ingenious speculation as to its uses. The idea, however, which seemed the most reasonable . . . was that therein, with right laudable and jealous care, I transported from place to place—my harem! . . . And great was the respect and consideration which this view of the case procured for me."

What actually went on inside the van was a tribute to Frith's patience. To meet the market's varying demands, many of the views had to be taken three times—with a stereoscopic camera, with a standard 8 x 10 camera and finally with a huge camera that used 16 x 20-inch plates. The temperature in his traveling darkroom went as high as 130° and more than once the collodion actually boiled when Frith poured it on his plates. But the demand for views of Egypt was seemingly insatiable and Frith set off on a second and then a third trip. In the summer of 1859 he went farther up the river than any photographer, and most travelers, had gone before: past the Fifth Cataract, some 1,500 miles from the Delta. The spectacular results of his three journeys through Egypt appeared in no fewer than seven different books. □

FRANCIS FRITH: *Aswan, Egypt*, 1856

Documenting a Way of Life

The ability of the camera to capture momentous events and romantic views was exploited from its earliest days, but photographers were slower to focus on the realities of life as lived by the people around them. The few who did use their cameras to document everyday society, such as John Thomson and Giuseppe Primoli *(pages 90-93),* left behind records that are now treasured. In their own time their work was barely noticed by the general public and an achievement in this field perhaps even more remarkable—Ernst Höltzer's detailed depiction of life in 19th Century Persia—has only recently come to light.

Höltzer was a German engineer who in 1863 signed up to help construct the first telegraph line across Persia —part of it a development program underwritten by the British to give direct communication with India and to open up new markets and sources of raw materials. Höltzer saw that the country was destined to be deeply changed.

In the 1870s, married to an Armenian girl and permanently settled in Persia, he became an avid amateur photographer. He spent his spare time recording his surroundings with an encyclopedic eye, paying attention equally to powerful rulers and the lowliest criminals chained in a state prison *(opposite).* He also took detailed notes on customs, professions, the legal system and practically every other aspect of his adopted land. However, he made no effort to publish the results of this labor of love.

In 1963, a century after Höltzer journeyed to Persia, his granddaughter brought several chests of his belongings back to Germany and stored them in a cellar. A pipe later burst and flooded the cellar. When the chests were pried open, it was discovered that the engineer had taken care to line them with waterproof zinc. Inside were several thousand glass-plate negatives in perfect condition—a precious and sensitive record of an entire way of life.

ERNST HÖLTZER: *State Prisoners in Chains*, c. 1880

Catching the Subtleties of a Vanished Society

ERNST HÖLTZER: *The Governor of Isfahan Province and His Son*, c.1880

Construction of the telegraph line took Ernst Höltzer to every part of the country, from the Russian border to the Persian Gulf. For a time he believed the people to be living in a state of near chaos. Riots and robberies seemed everyday fare and the Shah apparently had little control over local chieftains. "Persia goes along like some kind of drunken dreamer," he wrote, "and I must stand by and watch its grimaces." But as he grew more familiar with the people, he detected a dignity and orderliness that had supported Persian society for centuries.

The sultan at left, posing with his son, has a lordly bearing that seems completely natural and the Persian women on the opposite page display both the reserve and the stern strength that they actually possessed. Höltzer achieved these revealing pictures by avoiding the artifice that was typical of photographic portraiture of his day. Most photographers posed all subjects —whether they were laborers or noblemen—among the overstuffed furnishings of their studios. Höltzer, by taking pictures of people either in their natural surroundings or with plain backdrops, was able to catch some of the fine shadings of the Persian social order.

ERNST HÖLTZER: *Nun, Woman and Child*, c. 1880

Men at Work in Old Persia

The Persian activities were diverse enough to test the energies of a whole army of foreign observers, but Höltzer did an extraordinary job of taking it all in—from the sultan's bodyguards testing their marksmanship *(right)* to a barber at work *(opposite)*. In addition to photographing every aspect of Persian life, he made detailed statistical studies. For example, he noted that the province of Isfahan, where he lived, had "1,456 dyers, 35 bookbinders, 10 architects, 10 donkey-saddlebag makers, 200 Abyssinian female slaves, and 350 fine white servant girls."

Even athletes and entertainers did not escape his photographic survey. Almost every Persian town had a square where men came after work to do traditional body-building exercises or watch gymnasts practicing with heavy shields and other weight-lifting equipment *(overleaf)*. Höltzer's ubiquitous camera observed the scene and saved it all for posterity. ☐

ERNST HÖLTZER: *The Governor's Bodyguards*, c. 1880

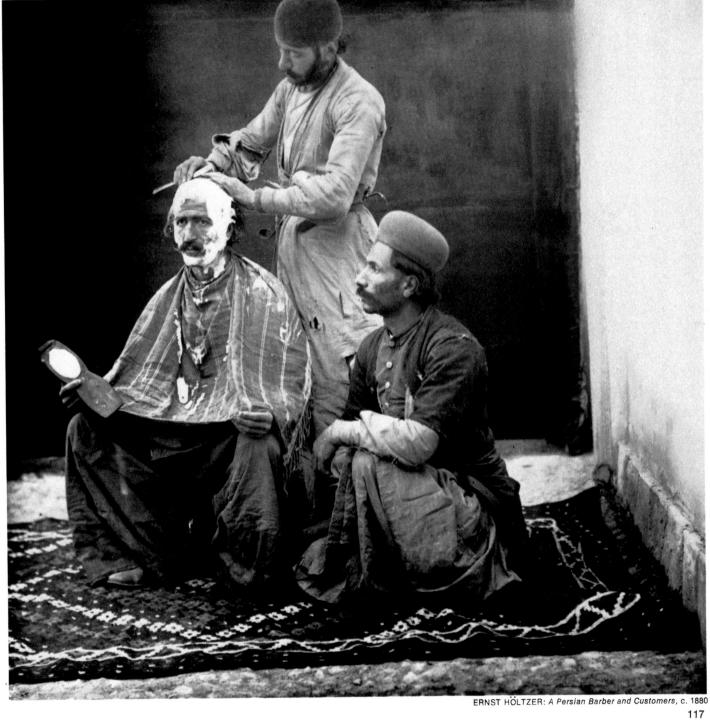

ERNST HÖLTZER: *A Persian Barber and Customers*, c. 1880

ERNST HÖLTZER: *Persian Gymnasts*, c. 1880

Modern Film **4**

EVELYN HOFER: *Composite portrait, using films of high speed (Royal-X, top), medium speed (Plus-X, center) and slow speed (Panatomic-X, bottom),* 1969

121

How Film Works

For photography, the advances in light-sensitive materials in the later years of the 19th Century were equivalent in impact to the effect of the automobile on the rest of civilization. Certainly the leap from clumsy plates to easily handled, factory prepared rolls of film was as great as the leap from horses to cars—and film pioneer George Eastman, like Henry Ford, saw to it that millions of Americans got aboard in a hurry. The first films were as cantankerous and slow as the early horseless carriages, balking whenever photographers attempted to capture a dimly lighted or fast-moving subject, but technology soon remedied that. Today, in terms of sensitivity, resolution of detail and other yardsticks of performance, modern films can run tight circles around their forebears.

Modern films operate on the same basic principles as the late 19th Century products. Light is captured by microscopic crystals of a compound called silver bromide (usually containing a trace of silver iodide). The crystals are carried in a transparent gelatin made from animal hides and bones, and this mixture, called an emulsion, is thinly spread on a plastic base that provides support. While these features have been around a long time, today's films are vastly more effective at registering light than earlier versions. For years manufacturers could not figure out why batches of film, all containing the same type of silver bromide crystals, showed wide differences in sensitivity. The secret seemed to be in the gelatin that held the crystals; it finally became apparent that the ability of film to record light depended on, of all things, the diet of the animals whose hides went into the gelatin. The hides of cattle that ate mustard plants produced much more sensitive film than those from cattle raised on other diets. In 1925 scientists discovered that the key ingredient contributed by the diet was a sulphur-containing oil from the mustard plants. Since then manufacturers have learned that there are many other compounds that affect sensitivity of films. Today, these are synthesized and added to the emulsion in carefully metered amounts to make batches of film of uniform sensitivity.

Another factor which affects a film's sensitivity is the size of its silver bromide crystals. An emulsion containing large crystals needs less light to form an image than an emulsion with small crystals. On the face of it, since high sensitivity is always desirable in photography, it might seem sensible for manufacturers to produce nothing but large-crystal emulsions. Unfortunately, there is a drawback: the bigger the crystals are, the poorer the image. A very sensitive, coarse-crystal emulsion will produce a grainy picture, speckled and lacking in fine detail. So, manufacturers offer a choice. A photographer can select a very sensitive but grainy film, a very fine-grained but less sensitive film, or a compromise between the two. It is not yet possible to have the best of both worlds, but some films come close to that ideal, combining great sensitivity with remarkable freedom from graininess. Today manufacturers have become so skillful at controlling the size of silver bromide crystals that they can now design a film with just the sort of characteristics they desire.

The usual way of describing a film is by its sensitivity or speed, indicated by its ASA rating—the numerical system, devised by the American Standards Association, that grades film according to the amount of light needed to produce a normal image. Higher numbers mean that a photographer can get his picture with less illumination (or can use a higher shutter speed to stop action). For convenience' sake, photographic equipment dealers often refer to films as being slow, medium or fast—slow being in the ASA 20 to 50 range, medium in the 100 to 200 range and fast in the 400 to 1250 range.

Photographers, quite naturally, crave simplicity and often rely on a single kind of medium-speed or fast film for all their pictures. One type may be insufficient, but just two—a slow, fine-grain one and a fast one—will do justice to almost any scene. It is frequently unwise to choose a fast film when it is not necessary to stop action or handle dim light, for a slow film usually yields a sharper, less grainy picture. The differences can be very significant indeed.

There is more to consider in selecting a film than simply its speed and graininess, of course. Some films are more sensitive to certain colors than others are. Early films recorded only the shorter wavelengths of light; modern films contain dyes to sensitize the silver bromide crystals to long wavelengths as well. They record the entire visible spectrum, although how closely they match human perception of the way the spectrum ought to look in black and white may vary from film to film. Some types can even be sensitized to very long waves the eye cannot see. And the instant-developing film of the Polaroid process provides unique effects of its own.

Film technology has come a long way. Sensitivity has been vastly increased, graininess reduced, and color-response broadened to include the whole visible spectrum. And many lesser problems of earlier films have been solved: for example, today's films contain dyes that prevent haloes from forming around highlights of a picture. Despite all these advances, the manufacturers may soon have to deal with a brand new set of problems, for radical types of film are in the offing. Since silver is becoming scarcer and more expensive, laboratories around the world are trying to find a means of recording images without silver compounds. Scientists hope to refine the quality of the electrostatic printing process—used in office copiers —enough so that it can provide the realistic images needed for photography. Other scientists speak optimistically of films that substitute nitrogen bubbles for silver in forming an image. Some sort of change is certainly coming, but the films of today will not be easy to surpass.

Making an Image in Silver

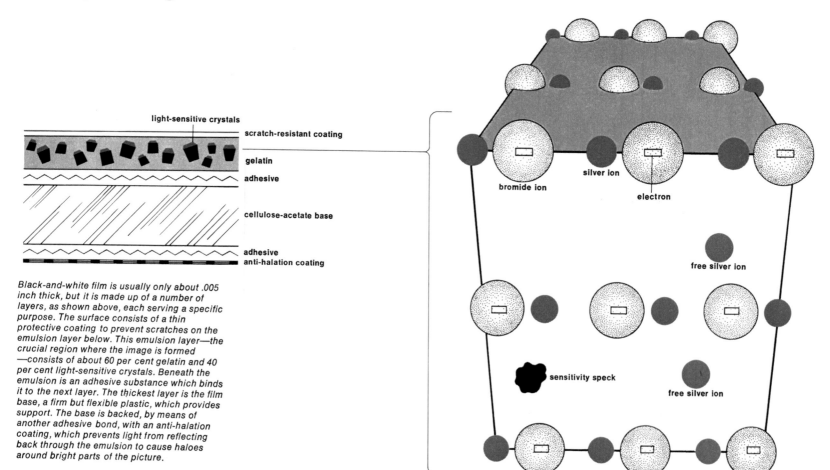

light-sensitive crystals

scratch-resistant coating

gelatin

adhesive

cellulose-acetate base

adhesive
anti-halation coating

Black-and-white film is usually only about .005 inch thick, but it is made up of a number of layers, as shown above, each serving a specific purpose. The surface consists of a thin protective coating to prevent scratches on the emulsion layer below. This emulsion layer—the crucial region where the image is formed —consists of about 60 per cent gelatin and 40 per cent light-sensitive crystals. Beneath the emulsion is an adhesive substance which binds it to the next layer. The thickest layer is the film base, a firm but flexible plastic, which provides support. The base is backed, by means of another adhesive bond, with an anti-halation coating, which prevents light from reflecting back through the emulsion to cause haloes around bright parts of the picture.

silver ion

bromide ion

electron

free silver ion

sensitivity speck

free silver ion

The process that creates a picture on a piece of film involves a remarkable reaction between light and the crystals spread through the gelatin of the emulsion layer. According to current theory, the reaction can be set off when one crystal—only about 40 millionths of an inch across—is struck by as few as two photons of light (a flashlight bulb emits a million billion photons per second). Each crystal is made up of silver and bromine; in the crystal their atoms are electrically charged—that is, they are ions that are held together in a cubical arrangement by electrical attraction. If a crystal were really a perfect structure lacking any irregularities, it would not react to light. However, a number of the silver ions in the average crystal are out of place in the structure and these are free to move about to help form an im-

age. The crystal also contains impurities—such as molecules of silver sulfide—that play a crucial role in the trapping of light energy.

As indicated by the diagrams on the opposite page, an impurity—called a sensitivity speck—and the out-of-place silver ions work together to build a small collection of uncharged atoms of silver metal when the crystal is struck by light. This bit of metallic silver, built up with the aid of light energy, is the beginning of what is known as the latent image; it is too small to be visible under even the most powerful microscope. But when developing chemicals go to work, they use the latent image specks of metallic silver in an exposed crystal as a sort of hook to which the rest of the silver in the crystal becomes attached, forming the image.

A silver bromide crystal (above) has a cubic structure somewhat like a jungle gym, in which silver (small black balls) and bromine (larger white balls) are held in place by electrical attraction. Both are in the form of ions—atoms possessing electrical charge. Each bromide ion has an extra electron (small box)—that is, one more electron than an uncharged bromine atom does, giving it a negative charge; each silver ion has one electron less than an uncharged silver atom does and is positively charged. The irregularly shaped object in the crystal represents a "sensitivity speck." In actuality, each crystal possesses many such specks, or imperfections, which are essential to the image-forming process (shown schematically at right).

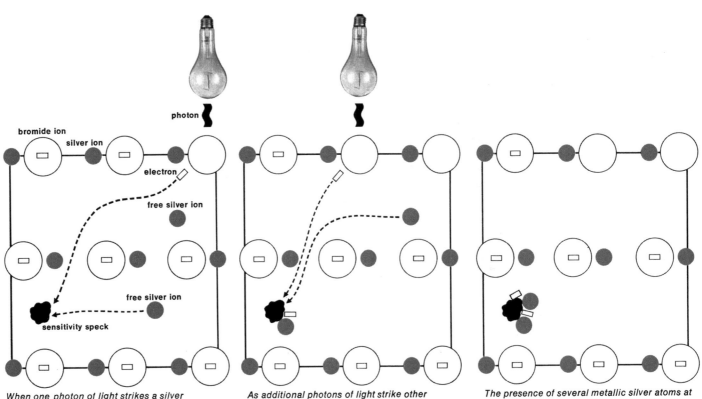

bromide ion
silver ion
photon
electron
free silver ion
free silver ion
sensitivity speck

When one photon of light strikes a silver bromide crystal, image formation begins. The photon gives its energy to a bromide ion's extra electron, lifting it to a higher energy level. Then the negatively charged electron can roam the structure of the crystal until it reaches a sensitivity speck. There, its electrical attraction pulls a positively charged free silver ion to it.

As additional photons of light strike other bromide ions in the crystal and release electrons, more silver migrates to the sensitivity speck. The electrons join up with the silver ions, balancing their electrical charges and making them atoms of silver metal. However, if the crystal were examined through a microscope at this stage, no change would be discernible.

The presence of several metallic silver atoms at a sensitivity speck constitutes a latent image —an invisible chemical site that will serve as the starting point for the conversion of the whole crystal to silver during development. The developer enormously magnifies the slight chemical change caused by light energy and creates the visible photographic image.

A negative is formed when millions of exposed crystals are converted to silver metal by the developer. The result is a record of the camera's view in which the film areas struck by the most light are darkened by metallic silver, while the areas struck by no light remain transparent after processing, since they contain no silver. The intermediate areas have varying amounts of silver, creating shades of gray that depend not only on the amount of light striking the film but also on the color of the light, the type of film and the way it was exposed in the camera.

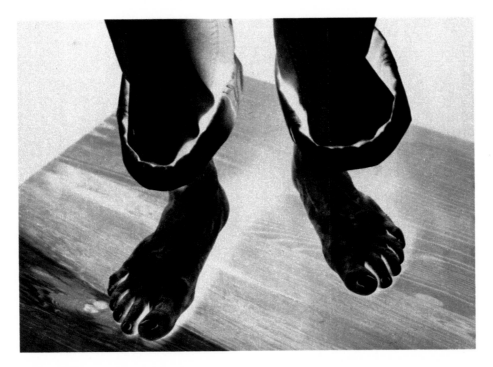

A Characteristic Response to Light

The pictures at right, all taken at the same aperture and shutter speed, seem to illustrate a truism about photography —that increasing the amount of light reaching the film causes a proportional increase in the silver density of a negative. As more and more light bulbs illuminate the head of Buddha, the negative becomes denser and denser. This, after all, is the very foundation of photography—the reason why shadows look dark and snow looks white in a picture. But the fact is, the density of an image does *not* always increase proportionally with the total exposure of the film. This fact has a profound effect on the way a picture turns out.

The response of every type of film can be predicted by its "characteristic curve," which shows how silver density increases as the amount of light reaching the film increases. The graph at right below represents the characteristic curve for the ASA 32 film used in taking these pictures. The middle part of the curve rises at an even rate—indicating that every increase in light, within this exposure region, will bring a proportionate increase in silver density. For good results in photography, both the greatest amount of light to be recorded (from the highlights of a subject) and the least amount (from the shadows) should fall mostly within this middle range of exposure.

If lens and shutter settings admit too little light, the film will react as indicated by the flat lower portion of the graph. This is underexposure; detail is lost because the film does not see the differences between light and dark at low light levels. Similarly, if the film is overexposed *(far right portion of the graph),* detail is again lost.

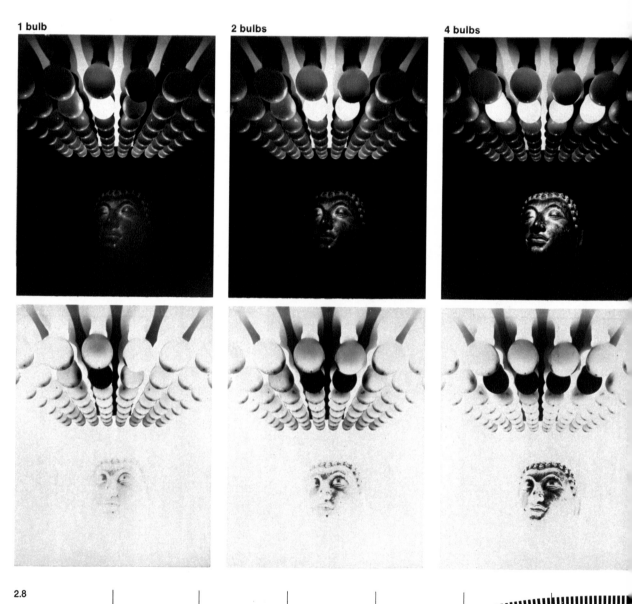

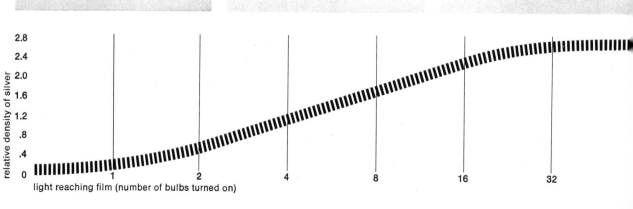

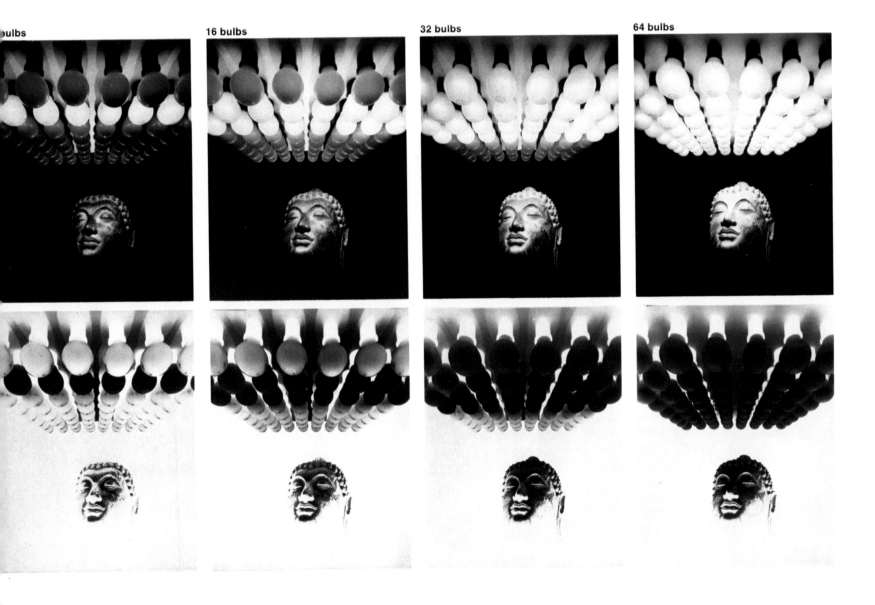

The Problem of Graininess

When it comes to light sensitivity and graininess, film gives with the right hand and takes with the left. The faster the film, the greater its graininess. Graininess is particularly obvious when a picture is enlarged. It reproduces gray shades not as smooth tones but as distinct specks; this mottling also obscures detail. Films containing large silver-bromide crystals produce coarser grain than those with small crystals, since they yield larger bits of silver when developed. (Actually, graininess is a result of uneven distribution and overlapping of many silver particles; the individual particles themselves are never visible.)

However, high sensitivity to light, or speed, *is* desirable—and in this respect the larger-crystal films perform best. This can be easily explained: a large crystal does not need any more light to form a latent image than a small crystal, but it will yield more metallic silver when developed. This bonus of silver is what makes it faster.

The relationship between speed and graininess is demonstrated by the photographs of a truck windshield below, taken with slow ASA 32 film, medium-speed ASA 125 film and very fast ASA 1250 film. Clearly, each increase in speed exacts a corresponding penalty in graininess. The moral is simple: if a photographer wants maximum sharpness and minimum graininess, he should select the slowest film that the lighting conditions and the motion of his subject will permit.

ASA 32 film

ASA 125 film

Enlargements from the pictures below show how graininess increases as film speed rises. The letter "G" directly below is sharp despite enlargement, for it was photographed with slow, fine-grain film. Some mottling and loss of sharpness is apparent in the middle letter, photographed with medium-speed (ASA 125) film. The letter at right, taken with ASA 1250 film, is severely speckled and its borders are unclear.

ASA 1250 film

What Happens with Underexposure

Photographers often find themselves forced to underexpose pictures; light may be too dim, stopping fast action may necessitate a high shutter speed, or the desire for great depth of field may require a small aperture. Considerable underexposure can be tolerated by most modern black-and-white films, and, in fact, parts of the picture sometimes benefit.

When a photographer intentionally underexposes a picture, he "pushes" the film; he simply assumes that it is more sensitive than it really is and arbitrarily assigns it an ASA number higher than the standard one specified. Then he sets his shutter-speed and aperture according to the pushed rating. Some compensation for this higher ASA rating must be made when the film is developed. Since the assumption of higher than normal speed provides less than normal exposure, the film must be developed longer to convert more silver bromide crystals to silver metal. This is a common procedure and manufacturers provide instructions that specify exactly how long to develop the film for different ASA ratings.

Despite compensation in development, however, pushing the ASA rating affects the image to some degree—as is shown by the three pictures at right, taken with a fast film rated at its normal ASA 400, then with the same film pushed to ASA 800 and then ASA 1200.

It is, of course, equally possible to rate the film at a lower than normal ASA number. This may be desirable when taking pictures in which the shadow detail of a scene is of major importance. Ordinarily, a different sort of developer is employed to compensate for such intentional overexposure of the film.

The bowl of roses directly above has been photographed with a fast film rated at its normal ASA 400. Since the negative is getting exactly the amount of light that the manufacturer intended, the detail in the picture shows up well, even in the shadow areas amid the flowers.

When the same film is pushed to a rating of ASA 800, reducing the amount of light that reaches it, details within the flowers are less visible. Something has been gained, however: because the shadows on the tablecloth are darkened, the picture looks more three dimensional.

Rating the film at a very high ASA 1200 causes a considerable loss of detail within the flower arrangement. Yet again something has been gained. The reduced exposure has emphasized the texture of the white tablecloth—which was a bit overexposed at the normal ASA rating.

How Black-and-White Film Sees Color

While silver bromide crystals are wonderfully sensitive to light, they do not respond to all wavelengths of light equally. This accounts for a paradox in photography: colors, or different wavelengths within the visible part of the electromagnetic spectrum, must be considered when making black-and-white pictures. Different types of film react to color differently, as the three pictures at right indicate.

Unless silver bromide crystals are specially treated, they respond only to the shorter wavelengths of light, from ultraviolet through blue-green. Photography got past this stumbling block back in 1873, when H. W. Vogel added a dye that extended the response to green and yellow wavelengths. By a mechanism still not completely understood, the dye absorbs these slightly longer wavelengths and transfers their energy to the silver bromide crystals. This sort of emulsion is known as orthochromatic, and is used today mostly to make photographic copies.

Other dyes now enable film to record all the colors seen by the human eye; this panchromatic film is the type almost universally used in ordinary photography. However, it does not respond to colors evenly. It is more sensitive to short wavelengths (bluish colors) than to long wavelengths (reddish colors). Unless this imbalance is compensated by filters *(pages 176 to 178),* blue sky tends to come out very bright, red apples are dark and even green leaves seem darker than they ought to.

Special dyes have also been devised to make films respond to invisible infrared wavelengths in addition to all the visible colors—with results *(far right)* that are eerie but often beautiful.

In a photograph made on orthochromatic film, some of the fruits and vegetables above come out looking darker than they would to the human eye, because the film responds only to shorter wavelengths—toward the violet end of the spectrum (above)—and is insensitive to reddish colors. The apple, orange and red pepper (upper right) and the red onion (lower left) all appear unnaturally dim.

When panchromatic film is used, the tones of reddish objects are somewhat more natural in appearance, because the film records almost all colors, red through violet and into the ultraviolet (above), that are seen by the eye. The egg looks even whiter than it does in the orthochromatic picture because it has added the light energy of the longer wavelengths to its blend of reflected colors.

Infrared film records visible colors as well as some longer wavelengths that are not visible. Although most natural objects strongly reflect infrared rays, there is no consistent relationship between the color of an object and the amount of infrared rays that are reflected. In the picture above, only the avocado and the mushrooms do not reflect infrared strongly; thus they appear darker than the other objects.

The Polaroid Land Process

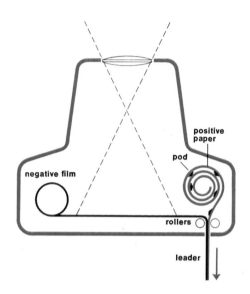

Some Polaroid Land cameras are loaded with two separate spools containing negative film and positive printing paper attached to a single leader. The negative is exposed simply by pressing the shutter, as in an ordinary camera. The leader is then pulled, drawing both negative and positive through a pair of steel rollers and out of the camera. The compression by the steel rollers ruptures a pod of jellylike chemicals attached to the positive paper, initiating development inside the sandwich. After 10 seconds or so, the positive is peeled away from the negative, revealing a finished picture.

When Edwin Land announced his first picture-in-a-minute camera in 1947, a major photographic equipment dealer dismissed it as a gimmick that would not last. Few predictions have ever been farther off the mark. Twenty years later, as many as 14 million Americans owned Polaroid Land cameras and the Polaroid Corporation was the second largest maker of photographic products in the nation. The "gimmick" had been refined to turn out high-quality pictures in only 10 to 20 seconds by taking advantage of a unique processing technique.

In the ordinary photographic process, film is exposed in the camera and later developed to produce a negative. Positive prints are then made in the darkroom by projecting light through this negative and exposing a second emulsion—the light-sensitive printing paper—which then must be developed. Polaroid Land film, however, provides both a negative emulsion and positive paper in one package. After the picture is snapped, the negative and positive are tightly sandwiched together. The image is transferred from one to the other by chemicals at the center of the sandwich, rather than by light. The positive image is formed with the aid of silver from the *unexposed* crystals of the negative—which would simply be washed away during the development of an ordinary film.

The way the camera makes a positive-negative sandwich is shown on this page and the chemical transfer of the image is illustrated opposite. In essence, the Polaroid Land process creates a highly efficient darkroom that is held in the hand for a few seconds, then thrown away when the work is done.

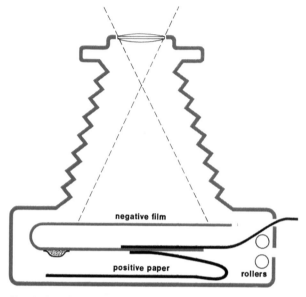

Most Polaroid Land film comes in pack form for easy loading. The pack consists of a box containing flat sheets of negative and positive materials, and is simply snapped into the back of the camera. First, the picture is exposed (above). The negative will then have to be turned upside down to meet properly with the positive paper. The photographer does this by simply pulling on a white tab (below).

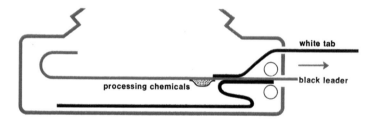

When the white tab is pulled, the exposed negative turns upside down and is brought close to the steel rollers (the positive paper has not yet moved). Next, a black leader is pulled, drawing both the negative and the positive through the rollers and breaking the pod of chemicals in the process (below). The chemicals are thus spread evenly within the sandwich to develop and fix the picture.

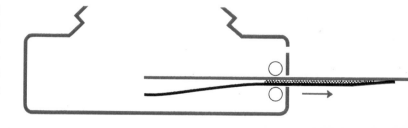

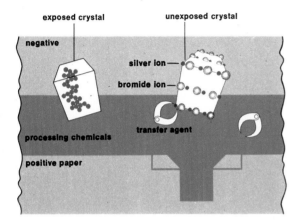

exposed crystal unexposed crystal

negative

silver ion

bromide ion

processing chemicals

transfer agent

positive paper

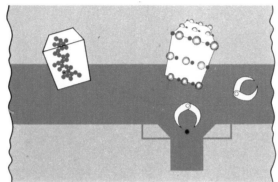

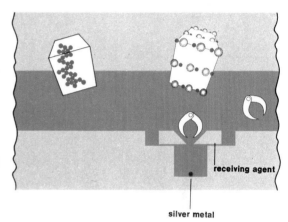

receiving agent

silver metal

When Polaroid Land film is developed, exposed crystals in the negative are reduced to silver metal in the usual fashion. But the processing solution also contains a transfer agent that acts on unexposed crystals. This transfer agent, represented by pincers above, latches onto the silver ions in an unexposed crystal.

After a silver ion is snatched away from an unexposed crystal in the negative emulsion, the transfer agent carries it to the positive side of the sandwich. Because the distance from the negative to the positive paper is only about .0002 inch, the silver ion travels directly across the gap, with very little sideways motion.

On the surface of the positive paper is a receiving agent, represented by a pair of sliding trapdoors, which acts as a catalyst and takes the ionic silver from the transfer agent—and at the same time changes the silver to its metallic form. The build-up of millions of silver atoms, in this way, forms a positive image.

Polaroid's Virtue: Speed without Graininess

The performance of Polaroid Land films is as unusual as their chemical means of making an image. While ordinary films generally suffer in graininess if they are fast, the Polaroid Land films do not. This behavior is demonstrated by the pictures at right, taken with Polaroid Land films rated at ASA 50, ASA 400 and ASA 3000. The main reason for the lack of graininess in all three of these pictures is the extremely narrow gap at the center of the positive-negative film sandwich that produces the Polaroid Land photograph. This permits the silver ions to travel in a straight line from the negative to the positive surface and they are less likely to form random clumps of silver, which are the chief cause of graininess and loss of detail.

Among Polaroid Land films, the ASA 50 film is unique in that it provides the photographer with a negative as well as a positive. (With all the other Polaroid Land films, the negative is always thrown away.) However, the negative is subject to the same laws of development that operate with ordinary films —that is, its graininess will increase with speed. Therefore, this film *must* be slow in order to yield a negative that will have a desirably fine grain. ☐

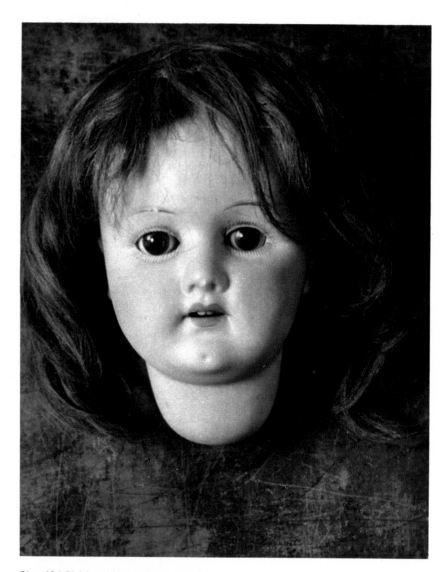

Slow ASA 50 Polaroid Land film produces grain-free pictures in 20 seconds—and also provides the photographer with a usable negative from which an enlargement, as much as 25 times original size, can be made. Other Polaroid Land films can be enlarged only by rephotographing the positive print with a camera to obtain a printable negative.

Medium-speed ASA 400 Polaroid Land film also produces a virtually grain-free image in 15 seconds. It is a good choice for general purpose photography. In addition, many professionals use this film for exposure testing, taking preliminary Polaroid pictures of a subject to make sure that the lighting effect is what they desire, before shooting with ordinary film.

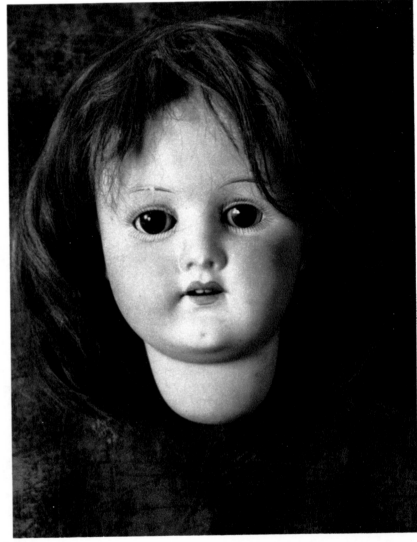

The extraordinarily fast ASA 3000 Polaroid Land film is remarkable not only for its great speed but for the fact that such speed is achieved without sacrificing grain quality. It is the most widely used of all the Polaroid Land films. It produces a 4 x 5 positive print in 15 seconds at room temperature; a longer development time is needed to get a good image in cold weather.

Fitting the Film to the Picture

Many camera stores stock a wide variety of black-and-white films ranging from very slow ASA 20 to superfast ASA 1250. Since faster films produce grainier pictures, a photographer will theoretically get optimum results by selecting the slowest film that suits each lighting situation.

In practice, however, it is inconvenient and unnecessary to work with a dozen types of film. Of the three general speed categories—slow, medium and fast—many photographers use a moderately fast film, such as ASA 400, for almost all of their work. This is possible because film manufacturers have made great strides toward reducing the grain problem in such high quality, fast films as Kodak Tri-X, Ilford HP4, GAF Super Hypan and Agfa Isopan-Ultra.

The portrait of actor Kirk Douglas opposite reveals the precision of detail, unmarred by grain, that can be obtained with a fast film—in this case, Tri-X. The picture was taken with a Hasselblad camera by Jeanloup Sieff, a French photographer best known for his fashion illustrations. Stopping down his aperture to f/16 at 1/60 second, he employed electronic flash to add brilliance to the highlights of the actor's face. The result was an extraordinarily intense close-up view in which every pore and whisker is sharply revealed.

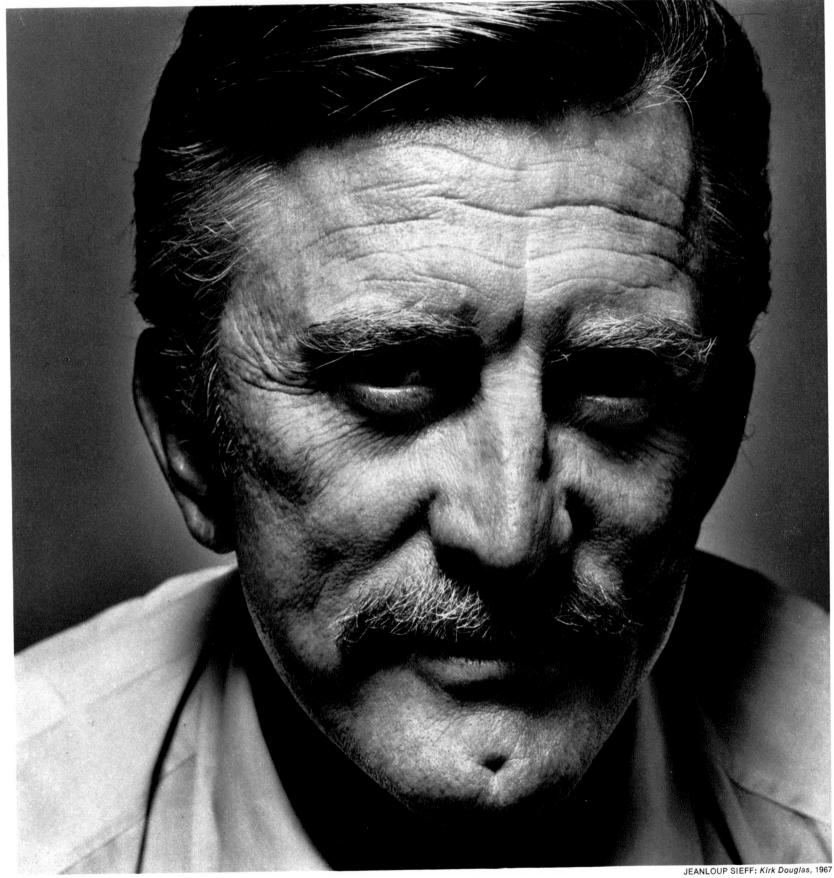

JEANLOUP SIEFF: *Kirk Douglas,* 1967

When Speed is Essential

ROBERT LEBECK: *Funeral of Robert Kennedy, 1968*

Modern fast films not only yield sharp, detailed images, but do this with light that only a few years ago would have seemed hopelessly dim. Even if pushed beyond normal limits and given a good deal less light than the standard ASA number calls for, these films can still produce a good image. German photojournalist Robert Lebeck exploited this trait of fast film when he photographed the funeral of Senator Robert F. Kennedy at Arlington National Cemetery in June of 1968. Using a 300mm lens set wide open and a shutter speed of 1/16 second, he exposed his Tri-X as if it were rated at ASA 1000 instead of the normal ASA 400 rating. In the solemn scene above, the pallbearers carrying

GARY RENAUD: *Motorcycle Scramble*, 1966

the flag-draped coffin are led by Senator Kennedy's son, Robert F. Jr.

With fast films' ability to cope with dim light goes their natural ability to stop rapid motion. When Gary Renaud took his picture of a motorcycle race at a dirt track in Pepperell, Massachusetts *(above),* he had to set his shutter at 1/500 second to freeze the swift action of the racers careening around the course. But the speed of his film—combined with the sunlight of a bright day— enabled him to set his aperture at f/11 for great depth of field. As a result of the small f-stop, even the grass in the foreground and the audience in the background of the picture are as sharply defined as his fast-moving subjects.

Making an Asset of Graininess

Certain photographs gain a misty, almost dreamlike beauty when rendered with a grainy texture. Fast films lend themselves to this effect more readily than slow ones because of the larger size of their silver bromide crystals. (However, any film will produce grainy images if it is suitably manipulated when it is developed.)

William Klein selected a fast film to create this grainy picture of workmen changing a street lamp near a Russian Orthodox church in Moscow. He shot the picture with a 300mm lens on a Pentax and intentionally overexposed it.

Overexposing a negative increases the amount of metallic silver in the negative and makes graininess more visible; it also allows the light to penetrate deeper into the emulsion, where it bounces erratically off crystals and further increases graininess. The combination of overexposure and enlargement of a 35mm negative produced a photograph with very coarse texture. Transformed in this manner, the clustered turrets, crosses and ornate lamp-fixtures of the scene become tantalizing echoes of the past seeming to reach the viewer across a wide gulf of time.

WILLIAM KLEIN: *Moscow*, 1961

143

The Uses of Medium-Speed Film

The all-purpose fast films become an inconvenience when shooting such intensely bright scenes as the one at right. For this picture of a fenced dune at Jones Beach, New York, free-lance photographer Melvin Ingber wanted to shoot toward the sun. If he had selected a fast film, the scene would probably have been badly overexposed—even with the fastest possible shutter speed and the smallest aperture. However, a medium-speed film (ASA 125) enabled Ingber to handle the intense illumination. He used Plus-X and took the picture with a Nikon at f/8 at 1/250.

In this case medium-speed film was also a better choice than a slow film, since Ingber wanted to catch the delicate shades of gray in the scene. This is more easily achieved with medium-speed and fast films, which exhibit less tonal contrast than slow films, and thus may be more suitable for photographing subjects that have deep shadows and very bright highlights.

Medium-speed film need not be limited to such marginal tasks as high-illumination photography, of course. It is an excellent all-around film, able to handle all but the dimmest light, capable of catching fast-moving subjects, and endowed with finer grain than the fast films. However, manufacturers are steadily improving the grain of fast films—and medium-speed film consequently seems destined for a reduced role in the future of photography.

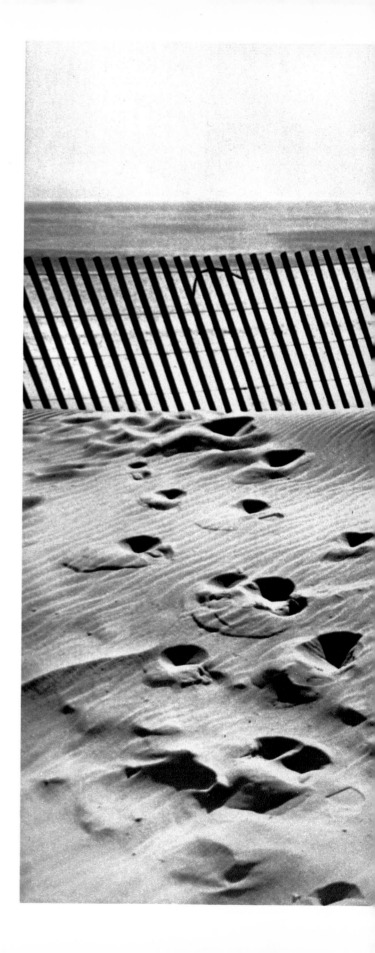

MELVIN INGBER: *Beach Patterns*, 1969

For Maximum Detail, Slow Film

A slow film, in the ASA 20 to 50 range, is photography's version of the old-style scholar—ill-suited to the dash and bustle of the world, but unsurpassed at working with tiny details. Its ability to render detail sharply is made possible by the small size of the silver bromide crystals and the thinness of the emulsion. (Thin emulsions reduce the internal reflection of light among the crystals—a bouncing that blurs edges.) The film is not very sensitive, of course, since there are fewer crystals in a thin emulsion and the small-size crystals yield less silver. However, if a photographer has bright sunlight or sufficient artificial light to illuminate his subject, slow film will allow him to make extreme enlargements of the picture without any sacrifice of clarity.

Slow film is a frequent choice for portraits—and the pictures at right, by Werner Köhler, a German freelance photographer, demonstrate its value for nature studies. Köhler's photographs were shot on ASA 50 Ilford Pan F film with a Leica equipped with a 50mm lens. Because the day was overcast, he set his aperture at f/5.6 and his shutter at 1/50 second. He captures such fine detail that the leaves and gravel look almost real enough to touch.

WERNER KÖHLER: *Patterns in Nature*, 1966

The Magic of Infrared Film

Infrared film can produce hauntingly beautiful outdoor photographs, giving the world a moonlit appearance—the sky dark, the clouds fleecy and the green foliage unexpectedly luminous. Minor White wrought this sort of transformation in his picture of a farm near Avon, New York *(right),* taken on infrared film with a red filter fitted to his Sinar 4 x 5 camera.

Most of the infrared films that are used for nonscientific purposes not only respond to some of the visible wavelengths seen by the eye, but gain their special qualities from their additional sensitivity to invisible infrared wavelengths that are just slightly longer than the visible waves of red light.

These "near-red" waves, emitted copiously by the sun and incandescent bulbs, create bizarre photographic effects because they are not always absorbed or reflected in the same way as visible light. When a deep-red filter is used to block most visible wavelengths, so that the photograph is taken principally with near-red waves, these

effects became particularly evident.

The leaves and grass in the picture came out snowy white because they reflected near-red waves very strongly (the surface features of leaves were lost, however, because the radiation was reflected not from the surface but from subsurface layers in the leaf tissue). The large water particles in clouds also reflected near-red waves quite strongly, making the clouds seem a brilliant white. But the sky turned out black, because its blue light, mainly in the short-wavelength range, was largely blocked by the deep-red filter.

Sometimes photographers use infrared film and a filter for long-distance views on hazy days. The haze results from the scattering of visible light by very small particles of water and smoke in the air—an action that does not affect the near-red radiation. Instead of being scattered by these particles, infrared waves reflected off the scenery can pass right through them as if they did not exist; a hazy scene caught on infrared film thus looks perfectly clear.

MINOR WHITE: *Cobblestone House, Avon, New York*, 1958

Polaroid's Limpid Tones

Polaroid Land film not only yields a finished print in 20 seconds or less, but it also achieves esthetic effects unattainable with ordinary film. Because the prints are almost completely free of graininess, they display an extraordinary creamy smoothness. The liquid quality gives the highlights of Polaroid prints a lovely ivorylike appearance. These virtues are apparent in the photograph of two ballet dancers at right, taken by Marie Cosindas. She used ASA 50 Polaroid Land film in a Linhof 4 x 5 camera, which was equipped with a special back to accommodate the Polaroid Land film pack.

Polaroid Land film has long been used by professional photographers as a kind of handy exposure meter. By using adapters to load an ordinary camera with Polaroid Land film, exposures can quickly be made and evaluated to avert a mistake when the picture is taken with standard film. Sometimes a Polaroid test turns out to be the final picture, as it did in the portrait *(overleaf)* of two women by Philippe Halsman with ASA 300 Polaroid Land film. ☐

MARIE COSINDAS: *Dancers Resting*, 1962

PHILIPPE HALSMAN: *Two Women*, 1958

Exposure: Key to Image Quality 5

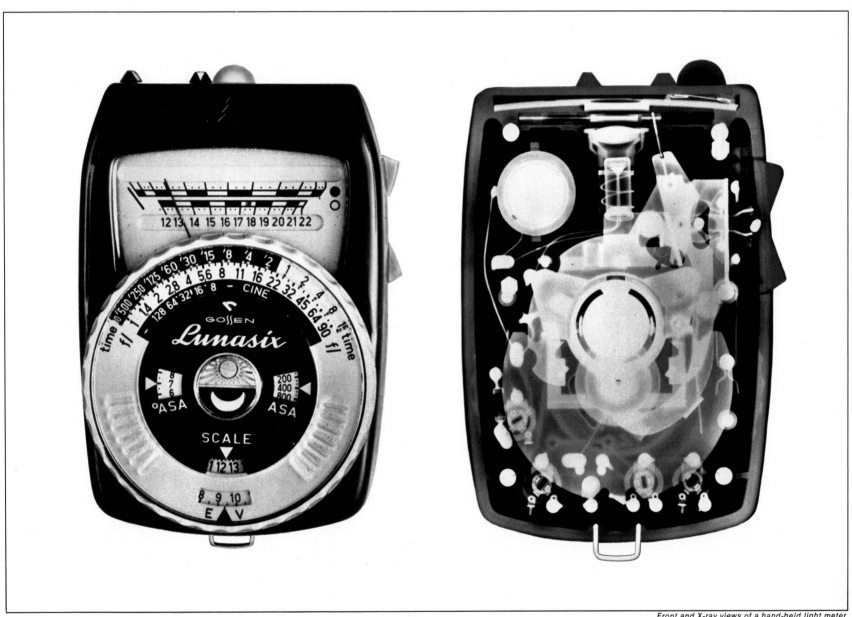

Front and X-ray views of a hand-held light meter

How to Expose for a Good Negative

In the early days of photography, there was a brief period when a photographer could see exactly how his picture was coming out at the time he was taking it. He simply watched the plate through a hole in the camera and, when a good image had been recorded, he stopped the exposure. Some professionals still determine the exposure needed for a good negative by the direct method of making test pictures (conveniently done with a camera adapted for Polaroid Land film). But most photographers rely on light meters and judgment. With films of standardized sensitivity, and with versatile meters to gauge light intensity, an experienced photographer can be almost as certain of getting the negative he wants as his 19th Century counterpart was when he actually observed the image forming inside the camera.

Setting the exposure is the final step—after film has been chosen and lighting is fixed—that determines how a scene will be recorded. In front of the camera is a world of rich and subtle colors, of a variety of textures, of strong and diffuse light—all to be translated, on black-and-white film, into tones of gray. The colors, of course, are lost. But with filters it is possible to control the exposure of black-and-white film to individual colors so that they can be distinguished one from another by differences in their shades of gray. Clouds can be made lighter than the blue sky, red apples a bit darker than green leaves, duplicating in gray tones the relative contrasts that color makes in nature.

But a photograph has only a limited number, or zones, of gray; at best, the brightest areas it records will seem 50 times brighter than the deepest black. Nature is far less limited. In an ordinary scene, some areas may be 200 times brighter than others, and the eye readily detects the detailed features in the darkest as well as the brightest regions. The photograph must compress this great range, and in doing so some details will be lost as the fine distinctions between slightly differing tones of gray merge into one. Which details are lost and which registered depends mainly on exposure.

Adjusting exposure for maximum detail is, to most photographers, the way to get a technically good negative. The explanation is simple: Undesirable details can be suppressed fairly easily later, during the printing process, but no darkroom legerdemain can supply details that are missing from the negative. To achieve maximum detail, the rule of thumb is: Expose for the shadows. That way the scene's darkest important features, reflecting the least light and producing the least silver metal in the developed image, are certain to be recorded rather than omitted entirely. Bright areas may then be so strongly registered that those portions of the negative seem blank patches of solid silver; rarely, however, are these overexposed sections as featureless as they appear, and much of their detail can be brought out in the final print by a number of darkroom techniques. Thus overexposure, while undesirable, is seldom as serious a defect as underexposure, and the time-honored exhortation "expose for the shadows" remains useful guidance. Also it should be remembered that most modern film has a considerable tolerance for overexposure. If the aperture is a stop or two greater than lighting conditions require, or the shutter speed is somewhat slower, the results are rarely disastrous. In most instances, the miscalculation can be easily remedied in the printing.

When time and circumstances permit, many photographers make certain of getting at least one optimum negative by "bracketing." One picture is taken at the apparently correct exposure, a second is made at one f-stop greater than the first and a third at one f-stop less. When he is ready to print, the photographer can select the negative that will give him the greatest tonal range in the finished photograph.

Getting a properly exposed negative is much easier now that photoelectric meters can be used to "take a reading" of the light falling on or reflected by the subject. Many different kinds of meters are now available, either as separate instruments or built into the camera. Meters vary, of course, in their degree of accuracy and in their ability to read low-level light, but almost any reasonably good meter will serve under normal conditions. For unusually difficult circumstances, specialized types are available. All measure light by the electrical reaction it causes when it strikes certain sensitive materials. Some built-in meters are interconnected to the camera's shutter and aperture, adjusting them automatically for the exposure without intervention by the photographer. More useful, however, are those—built-in or separate—that indicate their light measurements with pointers and scales, permitting the photographer to apply his own judgment as he interprets the reading.

Judgment is still necessary, even with the most accurate meter. For one thing, the area in the scene gauged by the meter may not be the one that is most important to the picture; the reading can then indicate an exposure that seems technically correct yet fails to produce a negative with detail where it counts. And for the finest results, the film's limited range of response to light must also be taken into account. Most scenes contain interesting details in many areas of widely varying brightness. The photographer must decide which are the most important and adjust his exposure accordingly; he may choose to forego the features in some dark sections in order to be certain of natural rendition of those in very bright sections—or vice versa. Only by careful study of the lights and darks in a scene can a photographer interpret exposure meter readings to get the kind of negative that will produce a good print: one with a full range of tones from pure blacks to pure whites, with a great many distinct zones of gray between the extremes, and with sharply defined detail in nearly all those zones. □

Light Meters and How to Use Them

The most important piece of equipment for any photographer who wants consistently accurate exposures is a good light, or exposure, meter. Light meters come in several basic varieties: self-contained instruments that are held in the hand; clip-on kinds that attach to a camera, and meters that are built into the camera itself. The built-in kinds are becoming more and more popular because they are so convenient. Yet many photographers, especially professionals, prefer the separate hand-held instruments, particularly when they want very precise control over pictures—for example, in doing portrait or architectural photography, when it may be necessary to set up a camera on a tripod and then be free to approach various parts of the scene and take light readings from close up.

The photoelectric light meters made today operate on one or the other of two light-sensing systems. The simpler ones employ selenium cells, which convert the energy of light into electrical energy that moves a needle across a gauge; the stronger the light the stronger the current and the more the needle moves. These have no batteries to wear out, but in dim light, where exposure is most difficult to estimate, the needle moves little or not at all.

In the other type the current comes from a tiny battery and flows through a cadmium sulfide cell, which acts as a resistor, conducting current and moving a pointer according to the amount of light striking the cell.

Light meters also differ in the way they can be used to measure light. Most hand-held meters—and all built-in ones—are of the reflected-light type, which measures the light reflected from the

subject. The meter is pointed at the subject—or at that particular part of the subject the photographer wants to measure at close range—and the reading is made. The light-admitting opening of such meters is restricted—by a hood, a baffle or a faceted lens—so that the angle of view of the meter approximates that of a normal camera lens, about 30° to 50°. In a variation of this type of meter, the angle is reduced to permit more accurate readings of particular parts of the scene. (In some "spot" meters this angle may be as little as a half degree.)

The second type is the incident-light meter, designed to have a much wider angle of view—about 180°—so that it can measure all the light incident on, or falling on, the subject from one side. It gains this wider angle by having a translucent hemisphere of white glass or plastic over the light-measuring cell to diffuse the light. The incident-light meter is held not toward the subject, but toward the light that is falling on the subject from the direction of the camera. Both types of meters generally are provided with two separate scales on the meter face, one to be used in average light and one in very dim light, so that accurate readings can be made under most conditions.

Since each type has advantages under certain circumstances, a number of meters, such as the one shown on the opposite page, are designed so that they can make either reflected or incident readings. When the sensing cell is open to direct light, as illustrated, it serves as a reflected-light meter; when the hemispherical diffuser is slid into position over the sensing cell, it becomes an incident-light meter.

A reflected-light meter (left) is aimed at the subject and measures the light bouncing off the man's clothing. The incident meter (right) is faced away from the subject and toward the camera to measure the general light falling on the man from the direction of the camera.

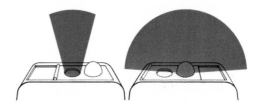

The opening in a reflected-light meter (left) admits light in a limited arc and therefore takes in a small area of the subject when used at close range. The incident meter's coverage, or angle of acceptance (right), is 180°, to enable it to measure all light coming toward the subject from the general direction of the camera.

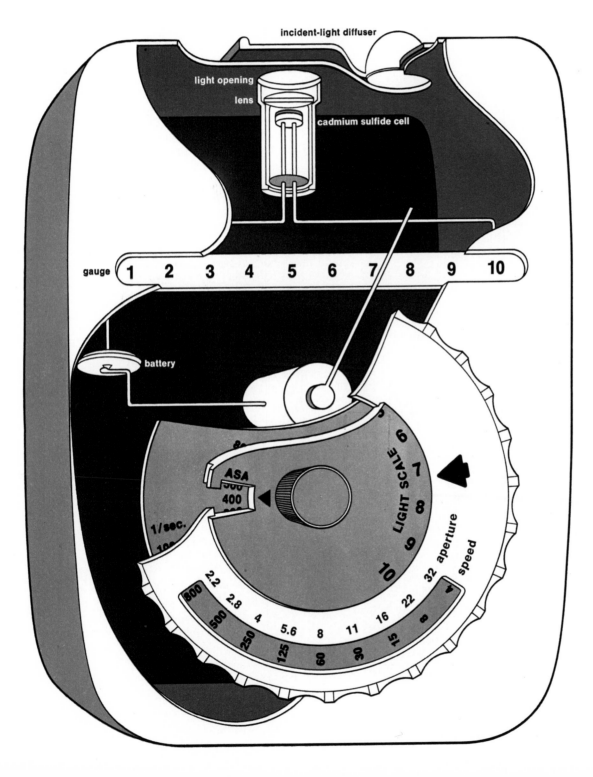

The meter at left is set to measure reflected light. The spherical diffuser, used to make an incident reading, has been slid away from the opening over the sensitive cell. Light enters the opening and passes through a lens to the cadmium sulfide cell. The cell controls the flow of electricity from the battery to a measuring gauge. How much light strikes the cell determines how much current reaches the gauge to move its needle; in this case the reading is slightly over 7. To convert this measurement into an exposure setting, the knob is turned until the ASA rating for the film being used appears in the small window near the center of the dials. Now the large outer dial is turned until its arrow points to the number that had been indicated by the pointer. This pairs aperture with shutter speed (appearing near the bottom edge of the dials) to give correct exposure for the light intensity measured. In this example, correct exposure would be f/2.2 at 1/800 second, f/2.8 at 1/500 second, or any other combination to f/32 at ¼ second.

The Incident-Light Meter

There are a number of photographic situations in which the incident-light meter, which measures light falling on the subject, and the reflected-light meter, which measures light reflected by the subject, are equally efficient. Former LIFE photographer Henry Groskinsky could have used either one when he photographed the church entrance shown here; in this instance he elected to work with an incident-light meter.

To take a reading *(left),* Groskinsky faced the meter away from the church and made certain that no shadow, including his own, fell on the spherical diffuser. This reading, taken at camera distance from the church, would have been satisfactory for an overall picture. But since he planned to photograph a side entrance to the church, where there was a strong contrast of highlights and shadows, he moved to the immediate areas to take readings.

Although there are many circumstances, like this one, in which the choice between an incident-light and a reflected-light reading is simply a matter of preference, there are conditions in which one or the other enjoys an advantage. For example, to determine an exposure for a distant subject, such as a city skyline viewed from across a river, the incident-light meter is usually more reliable. The reflected-light meter, which works well when readings can be made at close range, might be overly influenced by sky light and light reflected from the water. An incident reading is also likely to be more accurate in the photography of small objects against a brilliant background, such as tiny sea shells on white sand. The expanse of light area will inflate a reflected-light reading.

In the top picture, Groskinsky measures the bright sunlight falling on the steps and side of the church, pointing his meter at the light to gauge incident illumination. The needle points to just under 20 on the gauge. The exposure suggested by this reading produced the picture below. The highlights in this photograph are clear but the tonal range of the side of the building is limited; the shadowy area is grossly underexposed and all detail there is lost.

Groskinsky takes a second reading in the shadows beneath the portico (top) and this time the needle drops to 17, almost three numbers less than the one made in direct sunlight. If this reading were relied on for the exposure setting, it would lead to the picture below. The shaded areas are no longer black and the desired detail on the door is clearly visible. But the highlights on the steps and side of the church are now "burned out" because of overexposure.

To get a proper overall exposure, Groskinsky made a compromise between the two previous exposures, choosing a reading of just under 19 and setting his camera accordingly. This produced a photograph with good detail in the highlights, a broad tonal range and good detail within the shaded area as well (below).

The Reflected-Light Meter

The easiest way to use a reflected-light meter is to hold it alongside the camera and point it at the scene, as photographer Henry Groskinsky demonstrates at left. This procedure is generally effective if light and dark tones are of about equal distribution and interest; the meter indicates an average exposure that serves well. But if either light tones or dark ones predominate, the indicated exposure may fail to record detail in the minority tones.

The procedure followed by most photographers involves several readings taken from close range of different areas in the scene, dark and light, as shown at right. An exposure between the extremes indicated by the meter is then chosen. A simple average suffices in most circumstances, but, since detail is most easily lost in the darker parts of a picture, a somewhat larger than midway exposure is often favored if the shadow detail is particularly important or covers a large area.

Often light must be measured from the camera position. If the subject is the Grand Canyon, no one is going to climb the far cliffs to take meter readings. The same result can be obtained, however, by pointing the meter at nearby objects that share illumination and color with those in the subject and then averaging those readings.

This technique can even be used when taking pictures of people who are not easily approached for light measurement. Very often their faces are in shadow and an exposure based on a measurement of the entire scene from camera-side may make facial features disappear. The solution is to measure a shadowed face nearby—or even the skin on a shaded hand.

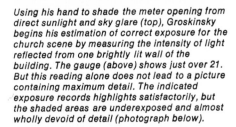

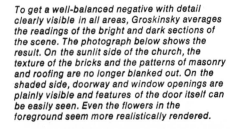

Using his hand to shade the meter opening from direct sunlight and sky glare (top), Groskinsky begins his estimation of correct exposure for the church scene by measuring the intensity of light reflected from one brightly lit wall of the building. The gauge (above) shows just over 21. But this reading alone does not lead to a picture containing maximum detail. The indicated exposure records highlights satisfactorily, but the shaded areas are underexposed and almost wholly devoid of detail (photograph below).

Measuring the illumination of the dark part of the scene (top) is also an essential step in accurate use of a reflected-light meter. With the meter aimed at a shaded section of the church wall (top), the needle on the gauge (above) points to about 17. But this indication is no more useful alone than was the one based solely on bright-area illumination. If it is used, the picture (below) is far from what the photographer wants. There is excellent detail in shaded areas but the highlights are nearly blank white.

To get a well-balanced negative with detail clearly visible in all areas, Groskinsky averages the readings of the bright and dark sections of the scene. The photograph below shows the result. On the sunlit side of the church, the texture of the bricks and the patterns of masonry and roofing are no longer blanked out. On the shaded side, doorway and window openings are plainly visible and features of the door itself can be easily seen. Even the flowers in the foreground seem more realistically rendered.

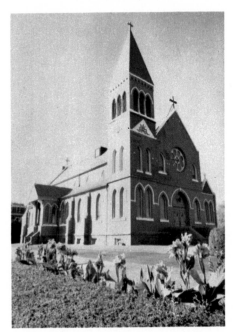

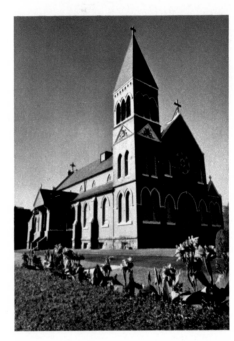

The Spot Meter

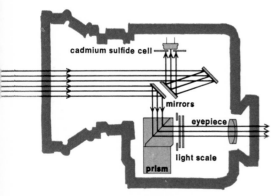

The operating principle of a spot meter such as the Minolta (below) is shown in the greatly simplified diagram above. Part of the light entering through the focusing lens is redirected by a mirror and prism to pass through the exposure scales and eyepiece lens, so that the photographer can aim the meter at his target. The rest of the light is reflected toward the light-sensitive cadmium sulfide cell. In front of the cell is a shield with a small opening, and this shield blocks most of the light; only the small fraction reflected by a small part of the scene gets through to be measured. The meter reading is visible over the scene as it is viewed through the eyepiece.

The spot meter also measures reflected light, but of only a minute section of the scene in front of it. Where an ordinary reflected-light meter measures light over an angle of 30° to 50°, a spot meter may measure only one degree or less. A specialized and often expensive tool, it is used primarily by professional photographers and advanced amateurs who want to gauge precisely the exposure required for one or more key areas in a photograph.

The spot meter is especially effective for obtaining readings of distant objects. The top picture on the opposite page was made with exposure settings based on a reading with an ordinary reflected-light meter. Because of the dark bushes and trees in the foreground, the reading was low and the buildings are overexposed. With an exposure obtained from a spot-meter reading of one of the distant structures, the picture (opposite, bottom) has excellent detail of the buildings and only a minor loss of detail in the foreground.

Looking through the viewfinder of the spot meter, the photographer sees a part of the scene (right) through a focusing lens that magnifies the image. A small circle in the center of the viewing screen indicates the precise area being measured. Around the edge of the viewing screen can be seen the two dials. The photographer sets the outer one, which bears shutter-speed markings, for the ASA rating of the film he is using. When he has the small circle superimposed on the area he wants to read, he presses a button and the motor-driven inner dial, which bears the f-stop markings, automatically turns to align shutter speeds and apertures that will give correct exposure.

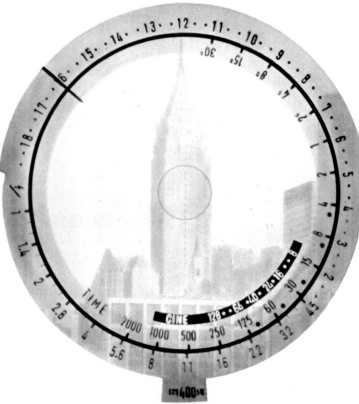

The spot meter's lens takes in only a small section of the photographic scene, but the image observed in the eyepiece is magnified four times. The actual area measured for reflected light (small circle) is a very small part of the visible scene, covering just one degree. To use the meter, a photographer sets the outer dial to his film's ASA rating (bottom), and points the instrument so that the small aiming circle is on the area to be measured; the inner dial then moves automatically to line up the proper aperture-shutter speed combinations. The short, innermost scale lists frames-per-second settings for motion-picture cameras.

Because of the dark foreground in the scene, an ordinary reflected-light meter gives an overly low reading, leading to a picture (top) with good detail in the foreground but little in the distant buildings. A reading of a small area of one of the brightly lighted buildings with a spot meter indicates a lesser exposure. In the picture taken at this exposure (bottom) the foreground is darker but there is good detail in the buildings.

Light Meters and How to Use Them: continued

Built-in Meters

The Averaging Meter

Although there are more than two dozen different kinds of metering systems built into cameras today, most of them are of the so-called averaging type. Like hand-held reflected-light meters *(pages 162-163),* they measure the average brightness reflected from all the parts of the scene in front of them and indicate appropriate exposure settings. The meters in most single-lens reflex cameras measure light that enters through the lens, as sketched in simplified form below, using two cadmium sulfide cells. This works fine for subjects in which there is limited contrast of lights and darks; but scenes in which very dark or very light areas predominate can lead to under- or overexposure if the meter is not properly used *(pictures, right).*

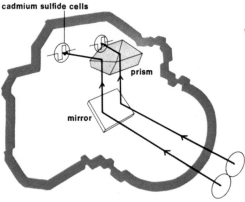

cadmium sulfide cells

prism

mirror

In an averaging-meter system in a typical single-lens reflex camera, light enters through the camera lens, strikes the angled mirror and is reflected upward to the prism. Cadmium sulfide cells are mounted on either side of the eyepiece and aimed at the prism; each measures light reflected from half the picture area. The cells are interconnected to give an average reading of light reflected from both halves of the scene.
To determine the proper exposure, the photographer generally watches a pointer or bar, visible in the viewfinder, and adjusts either the f-stop or shutter-speed setting. When the pointer or bar is centered or lines up with another pointer, the exposure is correctly set.

One cell in an averaging meter measures light reflected from the right half of the scene, symbolized here by the right circle, the other from the other half. In this picture, there is so much light from the large expanse of sky that the reading indicates an exposure setting one f-stop too small; the sky is properly exposed but the buildings have turned out dark and lack detail.

To determine the proper exposure for the buildings, light reflected from them should be dominant in the viewfinder when the reading is made. This is done simply by pointing the camera slightly down so that the meter's cells "see" less of the sky and more of the buildings, as indicated by the circles.

Having set the correct exposure determined by measuring the light reflected from the buildings, the photographer tilts his camera up once again, returning to his original composition. This time he gets a picture with a better balance of tones, revealing the buildings in good detail.

Because the areas measured by the cells overlap, as symbolized by the circles, the center of the scene accounts for a larger percentage of the measurement than the sides. Thus when an area of bright sky is at the center, the exposure indicated for the buildings is off even more than with an averaging meter—two stops underexposed in this case.

By shifting the camera so that a building is centered in the viewfinder, a reading appropriate to the structures rather than to the sky is obtained.

With the camera set at the proper exposure for the buildings, their details come out clearly; the sky is now somewhat overexposed, but since it has no detail, nothing has been sacrificed.

The Center-weighted Meter

On the assumption that most photographers place their main subject matter at or near the center of the scene, and want that area exposed for optimum detail, some camera manufacturers design meters to base their measurements mainly on light from the center area. Two cells are used, as in the averaging meter, but the parts of the scene they read overlap. In one camera, for example, the cells take 60 per cent of their reading from this center-weighted area (which is indicated by a circle in the center of the viewfinder); the balance of the reading is taken from the rest of the scene. If the central area is a patch of bright sky or dark background, however, this system, too, can lead to errors unless the photographer takes steps to correct them.

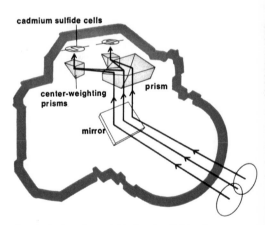

In a typical center-weighted meter, light enters through the camera lens, strikes the angled mirror and is reflected up to the prism, as in the averaging-meter system. To make the areas sensed by the cadmium sulfide cells overlap, a smaller prism is placed in front of each cell and angled in toward the center of the main prism. Because light from the center of the scene now reaches both cells, that area of the picture dominates the light meter's measurement. As when using the averaging meter, the photographer arrives at the correct exposure for his picture by adjusting f-stops or shutter speeds until the needle seen in the viewfinder is centered or matched with another needle.

The Spot Meter

The built-in spot meter, like the hand-held type *(pages 164-165),* measures the light reflected from a small area of the scene. The area being gauged is generally indicated by a small circle or rectangle in the viewfinder and, depending on the camera, ranges from 5 to 15 per cent of the total area taken in by the camera lens.

Because of the small area gauged by the spot meter, it must be aimed even more carefully than the other types. In the top picture at right, the area measured by the meter is once again a patch of bright sky and in the resulting picture the buildings are again underexposed. To get a photograph with detail in the dark areas, the exposure should be based on a spot reading taken of one of the buildings *(center).*

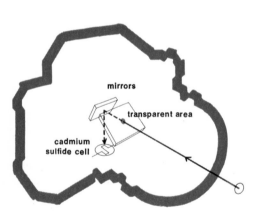

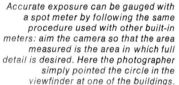

In a typical spot-meter system, light enters through the camera lens and passes to the angled mirror, which has a small unsilvered area in the center. Most of the light is reflected upward to the viewfinder; a small percentage passes through the transparent section of the mirror and is redirected downward by a second, smaller mirror to a cadmium sulfide cell. The cell senses only that small central area of the picture it is permitted to "see." In most cameras equipped with built-in spot meters the settings are made in the same way as with the averaging and center-weighted types, by adjusting f-stops or shutter speeds until the needle in the viewfinder indicates a correct exposure.

When a camera with a built-in spot meter is aimed at any scene, the photographer must be sure that the area covered by the spot is the one he wants to expose for. Here the spot, indicated by the small circle, covers the area of bright sky at the center. Since the measurement is being made entirely from this area, the buildings come out badly underexposed—by three stops.

Accurate exposure can be gauged with a spot meter by following the same procedure used with other built-in meters: aim the camera so that the area measured is the area in which full detail is desired. Here the photographer simply pointed the circle in the viewfinder at one of the buildings.

Having set the exposure for the buildings, the photographer returned to his original composition once more and this time got the picture he wanted

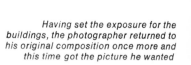

The Automatic Meter

The built-in automatic meter, which takes over the job of setting the camera for exposure by adjusting the aperture and/or the shutter speed itself, produces well-exposed negatives under average conditions. However, as illustrated by the top picture at left, underexposure is likely to result when the light behind the subject is extremely bright because the background dominates the meter's measurement.

In such a case the photographer can get a properly exposed picture by using one of several methods to "fool" the automatic meter. Perhaps the best way to influence the exposure controls is to alter the ASA rating set into the camera. By turning this adjustment to a rating that is different from the actual rating of the film being used, the exposure can be either increased or decreased. Use a lower-than-actual rating to increase exposure, a higher-than-actual rating to decrease exposure (with ASA 125 film in the camera, turning the setting to ASA 64 provides double the normal exposure).

Another way of correcting the automatic meter is to set the camera for a flash picture and place a dead bulb in the flash attachment, or, in some cameras, no bulb at all. This will cause an increase in exposure. ☐

The bright sky behind this girl will influence the light meter in an automatic camera to set exposure incorrectly; the girl's face comes out so dark (top picture) that none of her features can be seen. If the automatic controls are "fooled"—either by readjusting the film-speed rating to a lower ASA number or by inserting a dead bulb in the flash holder—the exposure can be increased to produce the accurate reproduction of the bottom picture.

The World in Tones of Gray

A light meter doesn't really gauge exposure. It measures light intensity. How that datum eventually determines exposure depends on how the photographer aims to reproduce on film the real world before his camera—a scene that almost always includes many colors of many brightnesses, all of which must be transformed into gray of several shades of brightness. Does he want the sunlit side of a building to appear as a blank white, or as a softer gray with some texture showing? How bright should clouds be? Should only a few tones be captured, or all?

Such questions are not automatically answered by meter readings. They require an interpretive analysis of exposure (often coupled with the use of filters). Such a sophisticated approach to exposure turns out to be simpler than it seems, thanks to the "zone system" developed by the noted California photographer Ansel Adams.

Adams' system is based on a printed "gray scale" like the sample opposite (they can be bought from most camera stores and sometimes come with exposure meters). Its 10 distinct shades of gray show the range of tones, or zones, that the print encompasses. These various zones can be compared—either from memory or from the actual scale —to tones in essential elements of the scene. Then exposure is set to reproduce those elements in desired zones.

The zones are numbered from 0, deep black, resulting from no exposure on the corresponding part of the negative, to 9, paper white, a dense section of the negative. Each succeeding zone (after zone 1) represents a doubling of the exposure of the previous zone—an increase of one f-stop. Obviously, the average tone in the average scene is a medium gray—zone 5—and in the average picture it should appear as zone 5. This is what all reflected-light meters are designed to accomplish; they indicate exposures that will reproduce as zone 5 any light intensity they measure. Only in the middle zones—3 through 7 —is detail clear.

How the zone system helps determine exposure can be seen in the picture opposite, on which numbers indicate the zones for various areas. The light shadows under the decks are zone 5 and a reflected-light meter reading of this area would have indicated the exposure for this negative. This exposure gave detail in the cloth cover (zone 2), but made the stairs (zone 9) too bright for clarity and the reflection of the hull (zone 1) too dark. Suppose some detail had been essential in the zone 1 reflection. By opening the lens one stop, the photographer would have shifted one zone up the scale, making some slight detail visible. But all other areas would be lightened similarly; zone 0 might disappear, and the zone 8 wall area would probably be indistinguishable from the stairs which are in zone 9.

This picture suffers no lack of detail. Its magnificent range of tonal values, 0 through 9, provides not only the accents of the extreme tones but also rich shades in the middle zones where the most detail can be readily accommodated. This full-scale rendition is generally the aim of the photographer, simply because it does make available more usable tones. But in some scenes only a few tones are of interest, and only they need be reproduced. The zone system can be used to interpret light-meter readings for either result.

DAVID VAN DEVEER: *Excursion Boat*, 1968

171

Photographing in Soft and Hard Light

MICHAEL SEMAK: *Italian Village*, 1962

To capture the mood of a softly lit scene or to present the dramatic contrast of hard light and deep shadows, a photographer often produces a picture with a severely limited tonal range. In the above picture of a lone priest on a fog-shrouded village street near Rome, photographer Michael Semak ignored the upper and lower zones of the gray scale and concentrated on the middle zones—from 4 to 7. For the harshly lit picture of a man on New York City's

Staten Island ferry, shown on the opposite page photographer Neal Slavin omitted almost all the middle zones and employed mainly the extremes—0 and 1, 8 and 9.

In each instance, the photographer deliberately sacrificed detail to get the desired effect. In the picture of the village street, the trees, except for the one in the foreground, are only ghostly shadows. There is slightly more detail in the ferry picture but the wall is com-

Because he wanted an underexposed negative, Michael Semak exposed for the average of all light reflected by the scene rather than for a dark object, recording the luminous fog as medium gray zones 6 and 7. Using a Pentax camera loaded with ASA 125 Ilford FP4 film, he made the exposure 1/125 second at f/5.6.

NEAL SLAVIN: *On the Staten Island Ferry*, 1967

pletely black and nothing can be seen outside the windows.

Both photographers could have included more zones of the gray scale, and still achieved almost the same effects by eliminating unwanted zones during the printing process. However, when the desired result is clearly seen, it is usually best conveyed if it is registered in the negative. Semak simply measured the light reflected by the fog, knowing it would indicate an exposure too small to record the darker zones in the scene; in this way he produced what would normally be considered an underexposed negative. Slavin also elected to make a deliberately underexposed negative, basing his exposure on the brightest zone, the light from the window. The long experience of the two photographers enabled them to visualize the negatives such underexposure would create, and in both instances the results are excellent.

Seeking limited tonal range and little detail, Neal Slavin adjusted his exposure to make the windows a blank zone 9, with nearly all shadows an equally featureless zone O. Only parts of the bench and the man's clothing are in the middle zones. The exposure was 1/125 second at f/11 on ASA 400 Tri-X, using a Leica M2.

Adding Tones by Adding Light

Both of the above photographs were taken with a Linhof 4 x 5 camera loaded with Tri-X film, which the photographer deliberately overexposed slightly. Even so, the dark areas in the picture at left remain featureless. To get detail on the shadowed side of the subject's face (right), a white cardboard reflector was placed to the left and slightly in front of him.

Under certain lighting conditions, a reflector or additional lighting is needed to broaden the tonal range and add detail. In the portrait above at left, for example, the highlighted half of the face is properly exposed but the other half is so dark—zone 2—that most of the detail is lost. Through the use of a white cardboard reflector illumination is supplied to the darker area, bringing it into the middle zones so that a considerable amount of detail appears.

Reflectors could not solve the problem posed by the scene on the opposite page. Because a small f-stop was desired to provide depth of field and bring all parts of the picture into clear focus, the illumination from room lights was sufficient only for the highlights *(top picture opposite).* A flash bulb to the left of the camera supplied light to bring most of the scene into the desired middle zones of gray *(center picture opposite),* but made the bright areas too bright. For the bottom picture, the lighting was not changed, but a faster shutter speed was used, darkening the higher zones of gray so that some detail can be seen in them. This also darkened tones in the rest of the picture, but enough of them remain in the middle range of the scale to give the detail the photographer sought.

The top picture in this sequence was taken with the kitchen's normal light (the exposure was 2 seconds at f/8 on ASA 125 Kodak Plus-X film in a Calumet 4 x 5 view camera). Only in the brightest parts of the scene—the higher zones of gray at top and right center—is any detail clear. Aided by one flash bulb, the same exposure (center picture) illuminated detail throughout, but shifted the bright areas to such high zones on the gray scale that their detail was blanked out. This was corrected by changing the exposure to 1 second, and the bottom picture shows details in both shadows and bright areas.

Changing Tones with Filters

The green filter *#58B, used to take the picture above at right, blocks out much red light and allows green to reach the film, making the red apples darker than the leaves, a natural appearance. Without the filter (above, left), the tones seem confusingly similar. To make up for light absorbed by the filter, the aperture is opened 2⅔ stops above the normal opening.*

Because black-and-white film records the world in tones of gray, dramatic contrasts in nature's colors are often almost indiscernible in a photograph. To the normal human eye, red apples are easily distinguished against a background of dark green leaves, but when photographed in black and white the apples and the leaves are reproduced in almost exactly the same gray shades *(above, left)*. Color filters are used to get a tonal separation that approximates the color contrast in nature.

Objects acquire color because they reflect part of "white" light—a mixture of all colors—and absorb the rest. Filters also absorb some of the colors in light, passing others. When the apples and leaves are photographed through a green filter *(above, right)*, the apples are considerably darker—i.e., less exposed—than the leaves because the filter has absorbed much of the red light the apples reflect but let the green reflection of the leaves reach the film.

Green filters are often used when a comparatively natural tonal separation is needed because they alter the exposure of film to red, making the relative difference between the two colors closely match those sensed by the human eye. To control the exposure of bluish colors, yellow or red filters are used, particularly for adjusting the tone of the sky. Film is so sensitive to the sky's blue and ultraviolet waves that even a dark blue sky causes about as much exposure as white would, and the sky often becomes nearly indistinguishable from clouds when photographed without a filter *(opposite, left)*. By using a yellow filter, which absorbs much blue, the sky is darkened and the smoke clouds become visible *(top, right)*. The contrast between sky and clouds can be made even more marked if a red filter, which blocks nearly all blue light *(bottom right)*, is used.

With a yellow filter #8K2, much of the sky's blue light is absorbed, making the sky in the picture at far right appear in its natural brightness (zones 5-7), somewhat darker than the smoke (zone 9). Without a filter (immediate right), the smoke can barely be seen. Because the filter absorbs some light, the aperture must be opened one stop larger than would otherwise be done.

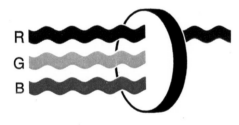

A red filter #25A absorbs nearly all blue and green light, making the sky in the picture at far right much darker (zone 3) than it normally appears and also darkening leaves and sand. Shadows, too, appear darker than in the unfiltered view (immediate right), for they are illuminated largely by blue sky light that the red filter blocks. Because of the large amount of light absorbed by the filter, the aperture was opened three stops larger than normal.

Eliminating Tones with Filters

Reflections from glass or water *(below, left)* are tones a photographer may wish to avoid in his picture. They can be eliminated very simply because they are made up of light that is unusual in that it is polarized; i.e., the waves are oriented at one angle rather than many angles *(pages 20-21).* This makes it possible to control them with a polarizing filter, which can block light oriented at one angle and thus also block the reflections *(below, right).*

A polarizing filter looks transparent but contains submicroscopic crystals lined up like parallel slats. Light waves that are parallel to the crystals pass between them; waves oriented at other angles are obstructed by the crystals,

as indicated in the diagram at right. Since the polarized light is all at the same angle, the filter can be turned to block it. This also blocks some waves in the general scene light, but only those oriented like polarized light; the rest get through.

To find the orientation that will block polarized light, the photographer looks through the filter and rotates it until the unwanted reflection vanishes. The filter is then placed in the same position over the lens. (With a single-lens reflex camera, the filter can be adjusted while it is in place over the lens.) Because of the partial blockage of light by the filter, the aperture must be opened 1⅓ stops above the normal exposure. ☐

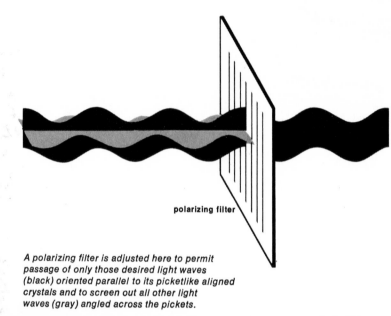

polarizing filter

A polarizing filter is adjusted here to permit passage of only those desired light waves (black) oriented parallel to its picketlike aligned crystals and to screen out all other light waves (gray) angled across the pickets.

HOWARD HARRISON: *Floodlights, Spotlights and Reflectors,* 1968

181

Basic Lighting Techniques

With modern fast films and lenses, no photographer has to wait for bright daylight to take his pictures. Even the ordinary illumination from lamps in a room is enough for striking shots *(page 184)*. But in many situations a supplementary light source can make a subject more fully visible, bring out the details in shadows, give an impression of three dimensions, or achieve special dramatic effects. Today there is a broad array of equipment and techniques to help the photographer gain these ends, from the flashcube that is popped into the top of a camera to the batteries of devices that sophisticated photojournalists assemble to light up an entire stadium at night or simulate a fire scene on a hillside *(pages 200-220)*.

These light sources are the fruit of more than a century of experimentation aimed at finding ways to make photographs any time, indoors or out. In the earliest days, getting enough light of any kind to record a recognizable image was one of the photographer's most frustrating problems. At first bright sunlight, and plenty of it, was the only real solution. All sorts of experiments were tried to hasten the agonizingly long exposure times, and to enable portraits to be taken indoors and on dull days. Among the first successful devices was an intensely flaming jet of oxygen and hydrogen gases heating a disk of lime to brilliant incandescence—the famous "limelight" used to spotlight actors on the 19th Century stage. In the 1850s came the discovery that burning magnesium wire produced an extremely bright light similar to daylight; photographers were soon setting off magnesium to record the wonders inside British coal mines, Kentucky's Mammoth Caves and even Egypt's Great Pyramid. The thick clouds of white smoke the magnesium produced, however, drove the cameramen choking into the open air after they had managed to get no more than one or two pictures. From the 1880s on, most artificial-light pictures were made with flash powder—an explosive mixture of finely ground magnesium, potassium chlorate and antimony sulfide that proved very effective but extremely dangerous. Whenever it was used there was always a threat of fire and many photographers and their assistants were burned or blinded by accidental explosions.

It was not until the 1930s that flash photography became simple and safe with the first mass production of flash bulbs, which looked like ordinary electric light bulbs but contained crumpled aluminum foil and pure oxygen that generated an intense light when touched off by a powder primer activated by batteries. Today's peanut-sized AG type bulbs, filled with finely spun zirconium wire, are the miniaturized end products of these years of effort. Flash bulbs are far and away the most popular source of artificial light among amateur photographers. They are inexpensive and very easy to use—particularly in the form of the flashcube, which contains four individual bulbs, each with its own reflector, built into one unit so that four pictures can be made in

The intensity of artificial light drops rapidly with distance. One foot away from the bulb shown here, a light meter receives 125 foot-candles of illumination; twice as far away, at 2 feet, the light is cut to 1/4, or about 32; at 3 feet to 1/9 or about 16. Thus the amount of light is inversely proportional to the square of the distance.

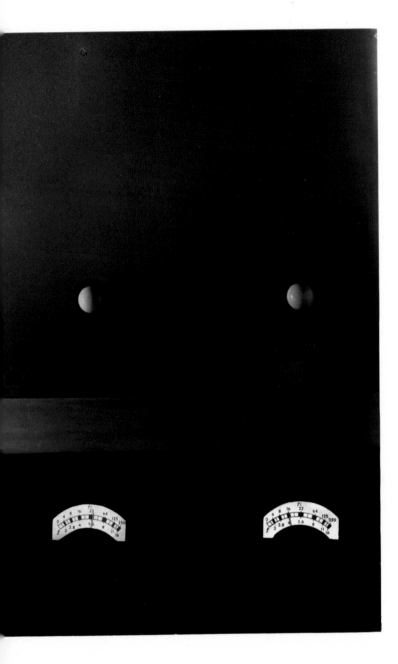

rapid succession. Cubes and bulbs are often mounted directly on the camera; while this restricts the choice of lighting angles, the limitation can be overcome and satisfactory results achieved with little effort *(pages 186-187).*

The flash bulb's glamorous younger cousin, electronic flash *(pages 190-191),* is an even more versatile and convenient light source. It, too, produces a momentary burst of light. But it can do so again and again as long as electricity is supplied, it is even easier to use than bulbs; and it is more economical for those who take more than a few dozen flash pictures every year. The idea behind the flash unit dates back to the beginnings of photography; in 1851 that doughty pioneer, William Henry Fox Talbot, fastened a page of the London *Times* to a rotating wheel and produced a readable image of it on one of his crude plates by means of an electrical spark from a battery of Leyden jars.

Today's electronic flash is less like a simple spark than like a small bolt of lightning. Electricity from batteries or a wall outlet is built up to a high voltage (as much as 4,000 volts in some units) and stored in the unit's circuits; when the switch is pressed this high-voltage electricity jumps from one electrode to another inside a glass tube filled with a mixture of gases such as krypton and xenon. The electrical discharge forces these gases to glow briefly and brilliantly with a color approximating that of daylight. The burst of light is so short—1/250,000 second or less in some specialized units—that it can be used to stop fast action, hence the alternate name "speedlight." Another frequently used name is "strobe," a hangover from the days when the newly developed device was first employed as a stroboscope—a light that flashes repeatedly at a controllable rate for studies of rapidly rotating machinery. The units now commonly used in photography are not stroboscopic; they produce a single flash each time the camera shutter is released.

A flash's short, bright burst of light is both an advantage and a disadvantage, for its illumination is difficult to control. Many photographers prefer to use flood and spot lamps when circumstances permit. Their continuous light is easily adjusted so that the pattern of illumination—the brightness and location of highlights and shadows—can be manipulated to suit the subject. The equipment need not be elaborate—many bulbs have built-in reflectors to concentrate or spread the light, and inexpensive sockets to hold them are fitted with clamps that grip shelves or moldings so they can be placed where required. (In addition it may be helpful to have a tripod to keep the camera steady in one position while lights are being arranged; it is also advisable to use a lens shade to prevent the lamps' direct light from shining into the lens.) The basic techniques for deploying such lights are simple *(pages 194-195 and 198-199)* and with practice one can learn to create pleasing illumination for indoor scenes and portraits.

Making Use of Existing Lighting

ELIANE GEHRI: *Man Drinking Coffee,* 1947

In a world heavily dependent on artificial light, there is often enough of it already in use to take pictures by. So before a photographer puts in a flash bulb or sets up a floodlight, he should examine the scene carefully; by using the available light he may avoid fussing with equipment, judge how shadows and highlights fall—and get a picture that will look more natural and authentic than one taken any other way.

The two pictures shown here demonstrate the point. Both of them capture the mood of a moment, which is largely created by the quality of the light: in one case the feeling of solitude and quiet suggested by a man sitting pensively under the warm glow of a single incandescent lamp; in the other, the impersonal look of a New York subway station, lighted by the cold glare of fluorescent fixtures. In both cases the light sources themselves are visible, becoming key elements of the picture.

GARY RENAUD: *In The Subway*, 1965

185

Six Ways to Use Flash

For most photographers, a simple flash unit—either bulb or electronic —mounted on top of the camera provides the easiest means for supplying needed light. An adequately exposed picture is almost guaranteed if the simple instructions that come with the unit are followed. But the trouble is that the picture almost always comes out flat, the subject two dimensional, with details bleached out by the head-on burst of light (broad faces are made still broader looking).

The fault lies not with the flash itself but with the way it is used. More natural-looking results, with a livelier, three-dimensional quality, can be obtained by employing such simple tricks as those demonstrated at right.

These techniques make any artificial light more nearly resemble natural illumination. Since almost all natural lighting—whether supplied by a window, a household lamp or a ceiling fixture —comes from above the subject, the most natural-looking pictures will result from a flash held above the level of the lens and slightly to one side or bounced in such a way that light comes from above. But natural lighting, indoors or outdoors, rarely strikes a subject from one direction alone; covering the flash with a diffusing screen, bouncing some of its light off walls and adding a second or third flash all help give a multi-directional quality to the light, creating the soft shadows, interesting textures and lifelike depth that most people prefer in their photographs.

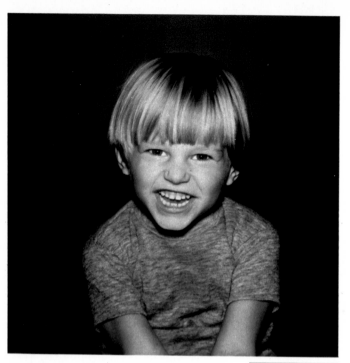

1. Direct flash on camera: For the majority of photographers, especially when they want to catch a fleeting moment, this is the quickest and simplest method, but the light is often flat and uninteresting, producing few of the shadows or textures that add roundness and sparkle.

4. Bounced flash: For soft natural-looking lighting, with good modeling of features, the flash unit (whether on or off the camera) can be tilted so that its light does not reach the subject directly but is reflected off a white or light-colored wall, as here, or a ceiling.

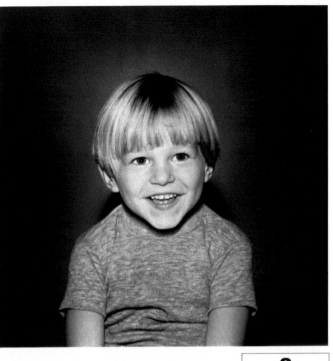

2. Diffused flash on camera: For a softer effect, the harshness and intensity of the flash can be reduced by placing a spun-glass filter in front of the unit, or by simply draping a handkerchief over it. This is a particularly useful way of preventing glary white features in closeups.

3. Reflectorless flash on camera: In some flash units, the reflector can be removed, allowing the light to radiate in all directions. Some light reaches the subject directly, but light reflecting off walls and ceiling helps soften the effect, lightening the shadows and adding depth.

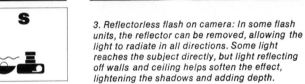

5. Flash off camera: When using a single light source, this is the best way to create appealing shadows and a three-dimensional feeling. The flash here is detached from the camera and held a distance of about a foot and a half above the camera and slightly to the right.

6. Multiple flash: This can give the subject maximum three dimensionality by making him stand out from the background. The main light here came from an extension unit to the right; a second flash illuminated the background; a third unit on the camera lightened facial shadows.

Avoiding Common Mistakes with Flash

The ominous shadow competes for attention with the subject in this picture. It could have been eliminated by aiming the flash so as to make the shadow fall into a position that is behind the subject or out of the picture.

It is difficult, particularly for beginners, to tell how the illumination cast by a flash will look until it's too late. The light's shadows and reflections are nonexistent until the picture is actually snapped, and even then they disappear so quickly they are hard to catch with the eye. The film catches them, though, sometimes with the results shown here.

Shadows are a particular problem, especially in close-ups of people, because they are very noticeable when a single flash is aimed directly at the subject (rather than bounced off a reflecting surface). It is difficult to make shadows fall naturally unless the unit is removed from the camera and carefully aimed; this sometimes means that the flash must be mounted on a separate stand, or that one person must hold the flash while a second works the camera.

Unexpected reflections of the flash itself frequently pop up from shiny surfaces: metal, windowpanes, a mirror *(right)*, the polished surfaces of furniture or paneled walls. If the subject wears eyeglasses, these may be a problem; they should be tilted slightly.

Flash illumination for color film calls for special precautions against "red-eye." This phenomenon is a reflection of the flash from the blood-rich retina inside the eye. It can be avoided if the subject looks away from the camera.

A flash held too high and too close to the subject casts deep, unnatural shadows, obscuring the forehead, the eyes and the chin. This error could easily be remedied by lowering the flash slightly and moving it to one side.

A reflective surface behind the subject—in this case a wall mirror—has caught the burst of the flash and thrown it back into the lens, causing a flaring "hot spot" in the picture. It could have been avoided by shooting at an angle to the surface rather than directly into it.

The Special Virtues of Electronic Flash

Because the electronic flash does away with changing bulbs after each shot, convenience is its most obvious asset. But it also offers a number of other advantages as a source of artificial light for the amateur as well as the professional photographer.

Most units today recycle, or regenerate themselves for another flash, in a matter of seconds, and they can be used to take series of pictures in rapid sequence—of the fast-changing activities and expressions of children at play *(right)* or the action at a basketball game. And because the burst of light is so brief—1/500 to 1/1000 second in the average unit—it not only is easier on the eyes than bulb flash (and thus less likely to startle or annoy subjects, particularly children and animals) but it also freezes all but the fastest motion regardless of the shutter speed that is used. With electronic flash it is possible to get such excellent action pictures as frame number 15 in the series shown here, even with a camera equipped only for slow shutter speeds. A sharp image of a fast-moving subject will not be obtained in this way, however, if much other light is present; at a slow shutter speed the existing light can form its own image of the moving subject, and this may appear as a blurred "ghost" image on the film.

The quality of the light produced by electronic flash is also an important virtue. Its color is very close to that of daylight, which means that it yields natural-looking results both indoors and outdoors with the daylight type of color film. Many photographers believe that electronic flash, properly used, reveals texture and tonal gradations more softly and naturally than bulb flash.

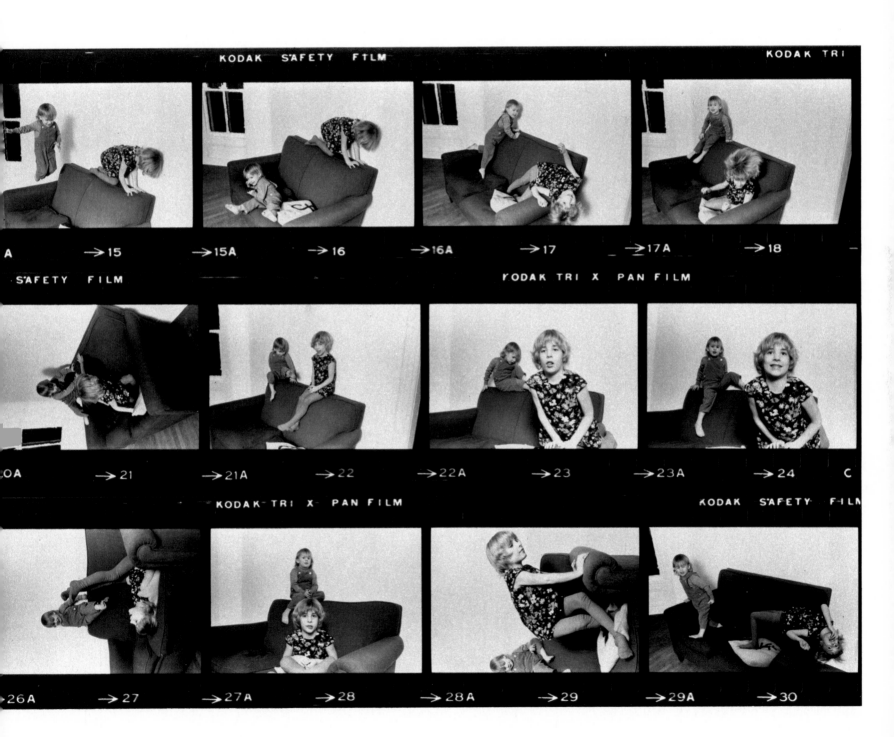

Floodlighting and Spotlighting

For quick, candid pictures in dim light, flash is the most convenient form of artificial lighting. But when a photograph can be staged—even informally in a corner of a room—a combination of floodlights and spotlights permits much more precise control over the result. Their continuous light can be turned on or off at will, making it possible to observe immediately the effects different lights and their placement actually produce and to control these effects by moving lights and reflectors around until the illumination is satisfactory. Proper exposure is determined easily and exactly with a light meter.

Floodlights and spotlights come in a variety of forms, including inexpensive

units with built-in reflectors that elimi-
nate the need for heavy equipment.
Most used is the floodlight, which, as its
name suggests, casts a wide beam of
light and can be used as general lighting for most subject matter, from room

interiors to close-up portraits, like that
of the cat at left above. A spotlight
throws a concentrated beam, producing smaller, sharper highlights, darker,
harder-edged shadows and a more dramatic effect. Although it can be used

effectively as the sole light source, as
in the picture above at right, it is generally an adjunct to floodlights, employed to emphasize a feature of the
subject or to add a bright accent to a
background or a person's hair.

Directing Light for Effect

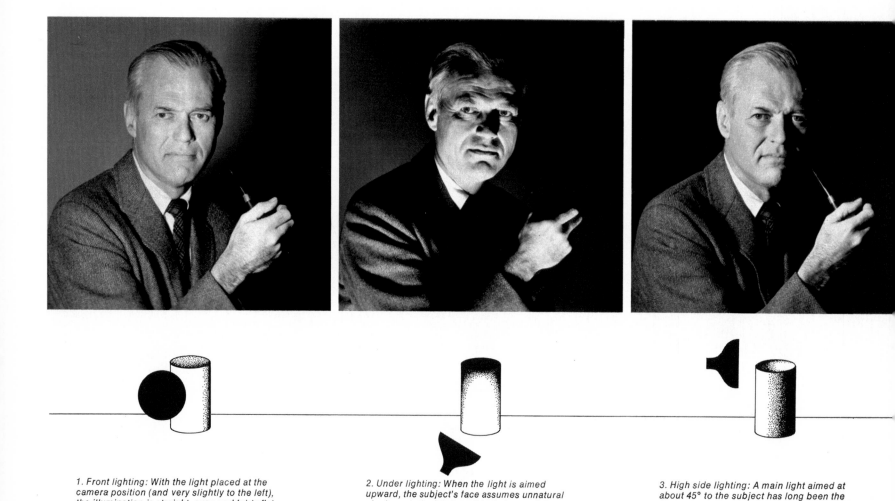

1. Front lighting: With the light placed at the camera position (and very slightly to the left), the illumination is straight, even and fairly flat, leaving thin, uninteresting shadows to the right of the nose and on the right side of the face.

2. Under lighting: When the light is aimed upward, the subject's face assumes unnatural shadows and a faintly evil look. In special circumstances this kind of lighting can be put to use to give the picture an aura of mystery.

3. High side lighting: A main light aimed at about 45° to the subject has long been the classic angle for portrait lighting, one that seems most natural for the majority of people. It models the face into a three-dimensional form.

In this series of six pictures of one man, photographer Henry Groskinsky shows how the position of the main light source influences the character of the image. For an actual portrait, Groskinsky would probably not use any one of these single-light positions alone (and would probably not employ the extreme lighting of positions 2 and 4 at all); normally he would add reflectors or secondary lights to brighten deep black shadows and create livelier detail for a more balanced effect, as is shown on the following pages.

Nevertheless, one principal source for light is generally necessary because we are accustomed to seeing things illuminated in this way by the sun, or by windows or indoor lamps. If, in a photograph, there are two or three equally important sources of illumination, arranged so that shadows and lights will criss-cross every which way, the result is visually confusing.

Since natural light usually comes from overhead, this is a logical location for the main source of artificial light. But very slight changes in the angle of illumination can drastically alter the overall result, and the exact position of

4. Top lighting: A light almost directly above the subject creates deep shadows in the eye sockets and under the nose and chin. In practice the light would be moved forward to lessen contrasts and illuminate the eyes.

5. Side lighting: Sometimes called "hatchet" lighting because it appears to split the subject in half, this type of lighting can be useful in emphasizing rugged masculine features or in revealing the texture of skin or fabrics.

6. Side-rear lighting: A light to the side and slightly behind the subject yields an even more dramatic effect. If the light were directly behind it would bring out the shape or silhouette of the subject and turn the hair into a halo.

the main source depends both on the subject and on the kind of interpretation to be given it.

For a striking portrait of a pretty young woman, some professionals use high front lighting—a cross between the positions shown in pictures 1 and 4 —because it provides straight-on, even illumination that results in an overall bright softness (especially if a diffusing screen is placed over the bulb) and it also is high enough to produce sculptured shadows under the eyebrows, cheekbones, lips and chin. For a woman who has less than perfect features, however, such shadows may be unflattering; they can be subdued with a secondary light source or partially eliminated by shifting the position of the main source down or sideways.

While overhead lighting generally gives a natural quality, side and low-angle lighting suggest mystery or drama just because they seem unnatural. A portrait of a weather-beaten family elder, for example, can be made expressive with side lighting—the positions shown in pictures 5 or 6—to bring out the strong line of a nose or chin, or the wrinkles that lend character.

Modifying Light with Reflectors

Although great pictures have been taken with a single flood or spotlight, most artificial lighting requires some modification to reduce harsh contrasts, bring out details otherwise lost in dark shadows and separate the subject from the background. The simplest, least expensive and often the most effective way of doing this is to use a secondary reflector to bounce the main light into areas where it is needed.

Reflectors come in many shapes, sizes and materials. All that most amateurs need, however, is what photographers call a "flat": a simple piece of stiff cardboard, about 16 by 20 inches, with a soft matte white finish on one side. The other side can be covered with kitchen aluminum foil that has first been crumpled and then partially smoothed flat again. The white side will give a soft, diffused, even light suitable for lightening shadows in portraits, still lifes and other subjects. The foil side reflects a more brilliant, "harder" light that tends to pick out surface textures.

No reflector: A single floodlight is positioned in front of the sculptured head, above and to one side of it (see small photograph above). The light reveals rounded contours but leaves the right side of the face hidden in dark shadow.

White reflector: A flat piece of white matte cardboard has been placed to the right of the head, held in a clamp stand and angled so that the light bounces back into the shadow areas on the right cheek and chin to lighten them.

Aluminum reflector: When the foil side of the same reflector is turned toward the light, the many facets of its crinkled surface bounce a harder, more sparkling light that reveals both the shape and the texture of the head.

Using More than One Light Source

It takes more than a floodlight and reflectors to do justice to a complex
subject like the ballerina executing a
croisé en avant at right, her arms out-
stretched, her head turned down, her
skin contrasting sharply with a costume
that almost matches the background.
To give each part of such a scene the
brightness it needs, most professionals
build up a system of several lights,
each of them carefully arranged to
serve a specific purpose.

First the direction, type and intensity
of the main light is decided on. In this
situation the photographer planned his
compostion around the linear pattern
formed by the dancer's arms, legs and
neck; a 500-watt floodlight, placed high
and to the front right, successfully de-
lineates all parts of this design except
the upraised left arm. That essential is
added with a diffused 500-watt "fill"
light angled downward from the front
left. This second lamp also lightens the
dark shadows cast by the first, so that
the ballerina's face, throat and legs appear in rounded detail. But she still
seems a cardboard figure. A 500-watt
spotlight, positioned high and to the left
rear of the girl, picks out highlights in
her hair and on the upper edges of her
arms and legs to suggest depth, and
also casts a clear shadow perpendicu-
lar to her body to emphasize horizontal
and vertical dimensions. Finally, to ori-
ent her in the space included in the
picture, a fourth light, a 500-watt spotlight, is placed to the right and behind
her to illuminate the backdrop. □

one light: pattern established

two lights: composition completed

three lights: depth added

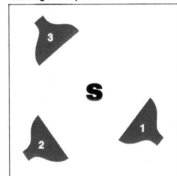

In the first picture (opposite page, at top), the photographer placed the main light on a stand 7 feet off the ground. The second, or fill-in, light (opposite, bottom) was placed at the same level as the camera, about 4 feet from the ground. The third, or accent, light (left, top) was placed high and to the left behind the dancer about 7 feet from the ground. The background light (left, bottom), used to separate the subject from the background, was set at a height of 7 feet.

four lights: three dimensions created

Wizardry with Flood and Flash

Today's sophisticated lighting equipment brings the world within photography's reach. It can illuminate an entire stadium for a night shot or light up the inner recesses of the human ear. But it can also help the photographer transcend the real world to create a surrealistic realm in which time, motion and space acquire new meanings, and even the contours of a head *(right)* reveal a unique view of man.

This picture resulted from a far-out aspect of space flight research. In 1954, when America's space program was in its infancy, LIFE photographer Ralph Morse spent 11 weeks with Air Force engineers photographing their efforts to prepare men for life in weightless and near-vacuum conditions. In one experiment to develop designs for flight helmets, the engineers were using a "contourometer," an instrument that measured the head and facial contours of large numbers of men. The device, which resembled a huge inverted horseshoe (visible at the top of the photograph), had a narrow slot on its underside through which a pulse of light flashed at intervals on each subject's head; as the rig moved from front to back, these stripes of light outlined contours that could be recorded by a camera for measurement.

Morse wanted to capture the bizarre over all effect, but realized that the light emitted during normal operation, though adequate for records, was too weak to make a dramatic picture. He loaded high-speed film into his Rolleiflex, set it on a tripod, darkened the room, and opened the shutter for a time exposure. Then he moved the rig over one man's head, a half inch at a time, permitting it to flash several times in each spot to build up the exposure. Despite these efforts, the first try was badly underexposed.

"We kept shooting and developing until we finally got one that had enough exposure," says Morse. "It took six flashes in each spot to register the light properly." The resulting photograph showed a strangely striped man who seemed to be the very embodiment of the eerie, unknown world that the first astronauts were soon to enter.

RALPH MORSE: *Space-Age Man,* 1954

A Whole Race at a Glance

While covering the Millrose Games in New York's Madison Square Garden, Ralph Morse hit on the idea of using a triple exposure of the 60-yard dash to show the beginning, middle and end of the race—all in a single photograph that would stretch time to make separate instants appear simultaneous.

To get the picture, Morse set up three pairs of electronic flash units. One pair was placed to illuminate the start, the second the midpoint, the third the finish. But if all three pairs went off together each time the shutter was clicked, as they would if hooked up by a standard circuit, the successive flashes would bleach out the images of the runners. To solve this problem, Morse made a special circuit-breaking switch that permitted him, with the help of an assistant, to operate each pair of lights independently of the others. The assistant was to set the switch to connect only the first pair just as the runners took off, then to switch to the second pair before they crossed the midpoint and finally to switch again to the third pair as the winner neared the tape. That way only one pair of lights would flash each time Morse pressed the camera's shutter release.

Having rigged his lights and wiring, Morse climbed up with his Deardorff view camera onto a specially built platform above the track. Using Kodak Super Panchro-Press Type B film, he set his shutter at 1/400 second, his aperture at f/11 and tilted his adjustable lens mounting, changing the optical perspective to keep the parallel track lines from converging too sharply.

To take the picture, Morse needed reflexes almost as quick as those of the sprinters, for he had to press his shutter three times within the 6.2 seconds the race took—and precisely at those instants when the runners came within the range of each battery of lights. His timing was virtually perfect, as the photograph at right shows.

RALPH MORSE: *Sixty-Yard Dash*, 1956

An Interplay of Lighted Images

Christopher Wren, the architect whose buildings transformed London after the Great Fire of 1666, had a genius for harmonies of design. When LIFE photographer Mark Kauffman set out to do a study of Wren's famous churches, he conveyed their harmony by combining several examples—widely separated in space—into a single photograph.

First Kauffman took Polaroid pictures of the individual churches and used them to compose his photograph in advance, cutting out the spires from each picture and arranging and rearranging them on a large piece of paper. When he had settled on the best composition, he photographed the building that was to be the centerpiece, the massive dome of St. Paul's, using a 4 x 5 Graphic view camera. By shooting at dusk, he easily isolated its bulk from its surroundings. Then he proceeded to photograph the other churches on the same sheet of Ektachrome B film. But to single out these smaller towers from their surroundings and make them stand out and against the dark central dome and sky in the final picture, Kauff-man had to light them individually at night, and this posed some problems he had not counted on.

In order to illuminate the church spires strongly enough, several 10,000-watt spotlights and a portable generator were needed. The London police gave him permission to set up these lights in the streets, but traffic and curious crowds made his work difficult nonetheless. To get a clear view of the towers over surrounding trees and rooftops, Kauffman took his pictures from a "cherry picker," a mobile scaffold of the kind used by utility repairmen. Each night Kauffman set up his scaffold and lights at a picture-taking site, but at least twice the preparations were in vain—a dense London fog rolled in and made work impossible. When conditions were right and the exposure was made, Kauffman moved on to the next site, sometimes to endure additional frustration. In the end, his labor paid off: the photograph of seven church spires, dominated by St. Paul's, suggests the "compleat Beauty" that Wren made his own goal.

MARK KAUFFMAN: *Church Spires of Christopher Wren, 1961*

Relighting a Fire with Flash

The catastrophic fire that swept through the fashionable Bel Air section of Los Angeles in 1961 left some $50 million worth of damage in its wake, a number of Hollywood stars homeless and a landscape reminiscent of a bombed city. The desolate scene was given an extra dimension by LIFE's Ralph Crane with an adroit use of flash bulbs, which he deployed to suggest an after-dark holocaust while revealing the devastation the fire left behind.

On a ridge overlooking a burned-out hillside, Crane set up two cameras: one a 4 x 5 Speed Graphic loaded with Polaroid Land film to make test exposures, the other a 4 x 5 Linhof view camera, with which he made the picture at right—10 separate exposures on a single piece of Ektachrome B film. Crane's two assistants, each carrying a hand-operated flash gun and a pocketful of powerful No. 22 bulbs, spread out along the rows of charred houses. They were alerted to move and to fire their flashes on signals from Crane, who blew a whistle every time he wanted them to move forward. When they had reached a spot that the photographer wished to highlight in his photograph, he opened his lens, then blew his whistle again as a signal that the flash bulbs should be set off. (The assistants kept out of range of the camera by taking cover in the rubble.) Crane made simultaneous exposures with both cameras; when he had finished he found two unlighted areas on the Polaroid print, so he sent his assistants back to those spots and made two more exposures.

Crane might have used portable electronic flashlights for his picture, setting off 20 or so simultaneously in different locations, but he decided that they would produce a relatively weak flash with too narrow a beam for the effect he wanted. By using powerful flash bulbs mounted in flat reflectors, he was able to spread a great deal of light across an arc of 180°. And with the flashes covered by red filters, each wide-sweeping burst of light created the grim illusion of an inferno still raging in the center of each house. By making 10 exposures of two seconds each, Crane provided enough light to be able to stop his lens down to f/11 for depth of field and still record the twinkling lights of Los Angeles that can be seen here in the background.

RALPH CRANE: *After the Bel Air Fire,* 1961

Using Light to Create Movement

BEN ROSE: *Model in "Motion,"* 1968

Repetitive flashes of light are often used by photographers to divide a motion into a series of steps that reveal the sequence of the action—the intricacies of a ballet dancer's rapid movements, the course of a curve ball as it speeds from the pitcher's mound to the plate. Photographer Ben Rose, on the other hand, sometimes employs the rapidly pulsing electronic flash in exactly the opposite way: to build up an illusion of motion where none actually exists.

The fashion models in the pictures shown here were photographed standing absolutely still against a black velvet background; their apparent motion is created in the camera. For the picture at left, Rose used four stroboscopic lights and adjusted them to fire at a rate of six times a second. His camera was attached to a special mount and an electric motor moved it sideways at an even rate. As the camera panned, Rose opened the shutter for about two seconds, a period during which the successive flashes exposed a series of some 48 images. For the picture at right, in which the girl seems to be moving toward the camera, he used a zoom lens and both zoomed and panned while the lights flashed on and off. The change in size of the figure in successive images is the result of the changing focal length of the lens.

BEN ROSE: *Style for Skiing,* 1969

Lighting for a Knockout

Suddenly the fight was over. Halfway through the first round in Lewiston, Maine, heavyweight challenger Sonny Liston lay motionless on the canvas. Towering above him in the referee's restraining embrace was the young, scornful champion Muhammad Ali (Cassius Clay), taunting his opponent to get up and fight. The knockout happened so fast that most of the crowd, including many of the ringside photographers, never even saw the shattering punch that put Liston down. But Neil Leifer of SPORTS ILLUSTRATED, anticipating a knockout—though not necessarily of the favored Liston—had been preparing for such a moment for several days.

Leifer's motorized Nikon F camera, which automatically advances the film after each exposure, was mounted on the framework holding the floodlights directly above the ring (the announc-er's microphone can be seen at center dangling from the same framework). The camera was equipped with an 8mm fisheye lens to take in a field of 180 degrees. Leifer's biggest problem was to provide enough light to cover the whole crowd and to permit the fast shutter speed needed to freeze the swift central action. He had assembled a set of 40 electronic flash units to supplement the arena's illumination system. Several flash units were mounted on the framework along with the camera; others were hung from the arena's ceiling.

Leifer chose his moment carefully, since he had to wait 25 to 30 seconds between exposures for the lights to recharge. He chose well. While shooting closeups with another camera at ringside 150 feet below, he had an assistant trip the shutter by remote control to catch one of the most dramatic moments in modern ring history.

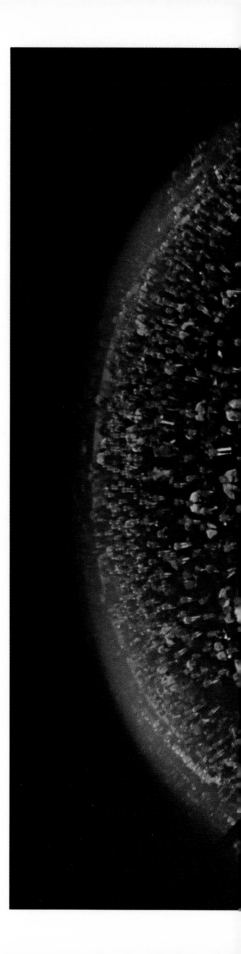

Total Lighting

Among the biggest lighting jobs to challenge the resourcefulness of LIFE photographers was the task of covering the historic visit of Pope Paul VI to America in 1965. Two of the high points of the Pope's visit were scheduled within hours of each other, one indoors, the other at an outdoor arena at night.

The vast, dim interior of St. Patrick's Cathedral in New York was the scene of the first religious ceremony ever conducted in America by a reigning pope. To get a color picture of the Pontiff's entrance Yale Joel needed every bit of light he could get. By placing 50 large portable electronic flash units around the upper gallery, he was able to create enough illumination to record the historic moment *(right)*. However, his use of almost all of LIFE's equipment meant that the next great event, a mass at Yankee Stadium, would have to be lighted some other way.

Ralph Morse, who drew the Stadium assignment, could count on one major assist. There was already plenty of light at the center of the scene, because the television networks had focused an array of powerful beams on the altar so that they could cover the ceremony. But Morse wanted to include a sizeable portion of the 90,000 onlookers in the picture as well, and he had to supplement the television lights with floodlights aimed at the crowd. To match the intense light at the center of the stadium, he was forced to use more than 100 lights of his own, mounted above the crowds in the dark areas of the balconies. His painstaking preparations were rewarded by a photograph *(opposite)* that dramatically conveyed the spectacle of thousands of worshippers being led by the Pope in prayer.

212

YALE JOEL: *Pope Paul VI Entering St. Patrick's Cathedral, 1965*

RALPH MORSE: *The Papal Mass at Yankee Stadium*, 1965

Blending Natural and Artificial Light

In the pictures shown here, photographer Arnold Newman balanced natural light and artificial light to achieve two quite different effects. For a portrait of the German industrialist and former arms manufacturer Alfried Krupp von Bohlen und Halbach, Newman sought to suggest the evil symbolized by this wartime master of slave labor. He posed Krupp in the grim surroundings of one of his factories. Daylight filtered in through grimy skylights and two spotlights (fitted with blue filters to match their color with that of the daylight) were placed low to cast harsh shadows on Krupp's face. To heighten the effect of the lighting, Newman took advantage of a characteristic of daylight color film—the tendency of its color rendition to be altered by long exposure time. The dim illumination called for an exposure of more than a second. That was enough to produce a greenish cast in the skin, adding to the aura of malevolence.

Newman's more flattering portrait of architect Louis Kahn *(opposite)* posed another delicate exercise in balancing light. Newman wanted to show Kahn against both the interior and exterior of his glass-walled art gallery at Yale University and decided to shoot the picture at dusk when the inside lights were on but the fading rays of the sun still lighted the façade. He chose indoor-type color film, which is color-balanced to suit both the colors emitted by the building's incandescent lights and the two spotlights used to illuminate the architect's face. It is not color-balanced for daylight, however. The result was a face warm and natural against the cool, blue-tinged background lighted by the rays of the fading sun.

ARNOLD NEWMAN: *Alfried Krupp von Bohlen und Halbach*, 1963

ARNOLD NEWMAN: *Louis Kahn*, 1964

Balancing Light in Two Worlds

LIFE's George Silk needed both ingenuity and luck to get this view of two forms of wildlife sharing a stream in Montana. He set up near the stream to photograph rainbow trout with a camera mounted in a partially submerged box with a glass front *(diagram below)*. But soon after he began work he noticed that a fawn came to drink from the stream every day late in the afternoon. He immediately saw the potential for an extraordinary photograph that would show fish and deer together. The light in the underwater realm of the trout, however, was far dimmer than that in the sun-splashed world above. In order to achieve a balance, Silk set a single electronic flash unit beside the stream and aimed it down on the water. He placed it close enough to the surface to make the illumination cast underwater match the quality of the daylight at the hour of the deer's visit. Finally, after weeks of on-and-off waiting, the lighting conditions and the animal participants came together. With high-speed Ektachrome in a Hasselblad camera, the shutter set at 1/60 second and the lens at f/22 (for maximum depth of field), Silk was ready. He recalls, "The fawn was a perfect actor—he walked over to the stream, drank and looked around, and I had time to take several shots before he disappeared."

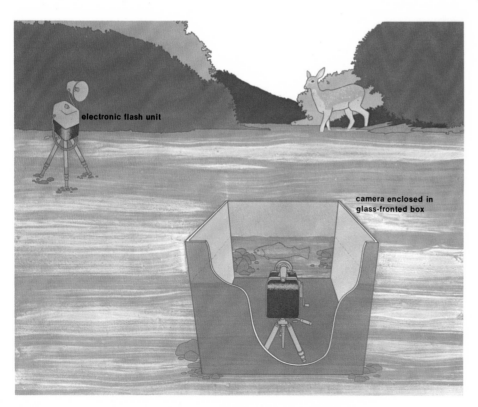

electronic flash unit

camera enclosed in
glass-fronted box

GEORGE SILK: *Fawn and Trout,* 1961

Capturing a Laser's Own Light

In the early 1960s the editors of LIFE assigned Fritz Goro to do a story on the laser beam, then just beginning to attract public attention for its potential in fields as diverse as communications and surgery. Laser light, unlike ordinary light, disperses relatively little, even over long distances, and thus can be directed with pinpoint accuracy. This precisely focused energy is now often used in operations on human eyes, to weld detached retinas into place, a technique perfected through experiments with animals.

When Goro decided to photograph a rabbit undergoing such an experimental operation, the scientists involved declared the task virtually impossible because of the difficulty in capturing the laser beam itself on film. Their laser consisted of a rod, made of synthetic ruby, that emitted a thin beam of red light when struck by the white light of an electronic flash tube. The beam lasted only a few thousandths of a second and Goro found that it could not be seen under normal laboratory light conditions. However, he knew the laser beam could be made visible by passing it through a field of smoke—if the smoke was of exactly the right density.

Goro had a special box built *(diagram below),* to contain the rabbit and the smoke. He then generated smoke by burning briquettes of incense and fed this into the chamber with a tiny blower. After dozens of test exposures, Goro found the right combination of film (fast indoor Ektachrome), aperture f/8, and smoke density. The result, seen at right, was one of the first photographs ever taken of a laser in action.

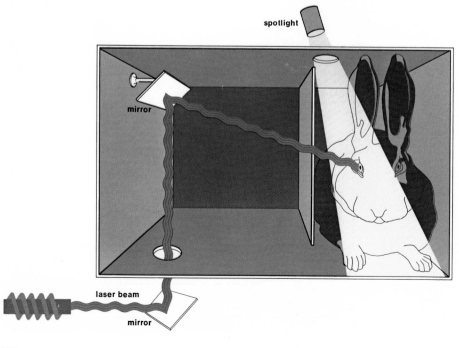

spotlight

mirror

laser beam

mirror

FRITZ GORO: *Laser Surgery*, 1961

Piping Light Inside the Body

Lennart Nilsson, a Swedish photographer renowned for pictures made inside the human body, has taken the camera's eye into such hidden realms as the womb and the twisting tunnel of an artery. One of his most exacting photographic forays was made into the middle ear—a region barely as large as a sugar cube.

The picture at right shows the ear from the inside looking out toward the eardrum. Taken during an autopsy, it reveals the exquisite engineering of the three small bones—called the hammer, anvil and stirrup—that transmit vibrations from the eardrum to a sensing organ. The picture was made with a tiny fisheye lens mounted on the end of a thin hollow tube; this lens projected the image to a second, larger lens, a half inch in diameter, that magnified the image 20 times and sent it onto the film.

To pipe light into the small cavity, Nilsson used flexible cords made up of many thin glass fibers. Light, picked up at one end of the cord, travels along the fibers much like water moving through a hose, and comes out the other end.

Nilsson used two cords, each carrying light from a 150-watt bulb of the type used in slide projectors; one was placed just behind the fisheye lens and the other on the outer side of the eardrum. To compensate for the slightly greenish light cast by the cords, he used a pink filter on his lens. Though not usually given to complimenting his own work, even Nilsson was impressed by the result, pronouncing the picture of the middle ear "unbelievable." □

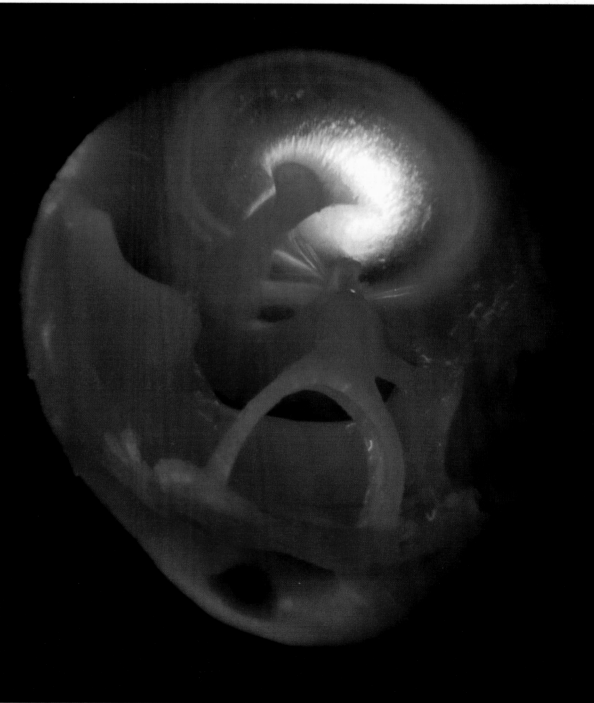

LENNART NILSSON: *The Middle Ear,* 1969

Bibliography

General
Feininger, Andreas, *The Creative Photographer.* Prentice-Hall, 1955.
Focal Press Ltd., *Focal Encyclopedia of Photography.* McGraw-Hill, 1959.
Neblette, Carroll B., *Photography: Its Materials and Processes.* Van Nostrand, 1962.
Rhode, Robert B., and Floyd H. McCall, *Introduction to Photography.* Macmillan, 1965.
Sussman, Aaron, *The Amateur Photographer's Handbook.* Thomas Y. Crowell, 1965.

History
Darrah, William Culp, *Stereo Views: A History of Stereographs in America and Their Collection.* Times and News Publishing, 1964.
*Eder, Josef Maria, *History of Photography.* Columbia University Press, 1945.
Gardner, Alexander, *Gardner's Photographic Sketch Book of the Civil War.* Dover Publications, 1959.
Gernsheim, Helmut, *History of Photography.* Oxford University Press, 1955.
Gernsheim, Helmut, and Alison, *L.J.M. Daguerre: The History of the Diorama and the Daguerreotype.* Secker and Warburg, 1956.
Newhall, Beaumont:
  The Daguerreotype in America. Duell, Sloan and Pearce, 1961.
  The History of Photography from 1839 to the Present Day. The Museum of Modern Art, Doubleday, 1964.
Pollack, Peter, *The Picture History of Photography.* Harry N. Abrams, 1958.
†Taft, Robert, *Photography and the American Scene.* Dover Publications, 1964.

Biography
Barnett, Lincoln, *The Universe and Dr. Einstein.* William Sloane Associates, 1948.
Gernsheim, Helmut, and Alison, *Roger Fenton, Photographer of the Crimean War.* Secker and Warburg, 1954.
Horan, James D.:
  Mathew Brady, Historian with a Camera. Crown Publishers, 1955.
  Timothy O'Sullivan, America's Forgotten Photographer. Doubleday, 1966.
Jackson, Clarence S., *Picture Maker of the Old West, William H. Jackson.* Scribner, 1947.

Special Fields
Adams, Ansel:
  Polaroid Land Photography Manual. Morgan & Morgan, 1963.
  The Negative. Morgan & Morgan, 1968.
Eastman Kodak:
  †*Applied Infrared Photography.* Eastman Kodak, 1968.
  Filters for Black and White and Color Pictures. Eastman Kodak, 1969.
  Flash Pictures. Eastman Kodak, 1967.
  †*Kodak Black-and-White Films in Rolls.* Eastman Kodak, 1967.
Eaton, George T., *Photographic Chemistry.* Morgan & Morgan, 1965.
Hackforth, Henry L., *Infrared Radiation.* McGraw-Hill, 1960.
Jacobs, Lou Jr., *Electronic Flash.* American Photographic Book Publishing Co., 1962.
Massy, H.S.W., and R.L.F. Boyd, *The Upper Atmosphere.* Philosophical Library, 1958.
Mees, C.E. Kenneth, *From Dry Plates to Ektachrome Film.* Ziff-Davis, 1961.

Mees, C.E. Kenneth, and T.H. James, *The Theory of the Photographic Process.* Macmillan, 1966.
Mueller, Conrad G., and Mae Rudolph and the Editors of TIME-LIFE Books, *Light and Vision.* TIME-LIFE Books, 1969.
Newhall, Beaumont, *Airborne Camera, The World from the Air and Outer Space.* Hastings House, 1969.
Smith, Alpheus W., and John N. Cooper, *Elements of Physics.* McGraw-Hill, 1964.
White, Minor, *The Zone System Manual.* Morgan & Morgan, 1968.

Magazines
Aperture, Aperture Inc., New York City
British Journal of Photography, Henry Greenwood and Co., London
Camera, C.J. Bucher Ltd., Lucerne, Switzerland
Camera 35, U.S. Camera Publishing Co., New York City
Creative Camera, International Federation of Amateur Photographers, London
Infinity, American Society of Magazine Photographers, New York City
Modern Photography, The Billboard Publishing Co., New York City
Popular Photography, Ziff-Davis Publishing Co., New York City
Travel & Camera, U.S. Camera Publishing Corp., New York City
U.S. Camera World Annual, U.S. Camera Publishing Corp., New York City

*Also available in paperback.
†Available only in paperback.

Acknowledgments

For help given in the preparation of this book, the editors are indebted to Myles Adler, Public Relations Department, AGFA-Gevaert, Inc., Teterboro, New Jersey; Photography Archives, Art Institute of Chicago, Chicago, Illinois; Norbert S. Baer, Institute of Fine Arts, New York University, New York City; Samuel Berkey, President, Berkey Photo, Inc., New York City; Richard O. Berube, Publicity Department, Polaroid Corporation, Cambridge, Massachusetts; Robert E. Bilbey, Manager, Advertising and Sales Promotion Department and Richard Craig, Aerospace Product Specialist, Weston Instruments, Inc., Newark, New Jersey; Priscilla Bresbery, Society of Illuminating Engineers, New York City; Josephine Cobb, Specialist in Iconography, General Services Administration, National Archives and Records Service, Washington, D.C.; Glen F. Cruze, Application Engineer, Mallory Battery Co., Tarrytown, New York; Peter Denzer, Brooklyn, New York; Stanley Erinwein, Tiffen Manufacturing Corp., Roslyn Heights, New York; George Eastman House, Rochester, New York; Fritz Goro, Chappaqua, New York; David Haberstich, Museum Specialist, Section of Photography, The Smithsonian Institution, Washington, D.C.; James Hartnett, Supervisor, Photographic Service Department, Polaroid Corp., Cambridge, Massachusetts; James D. Horan, Weehawken, New Jersey; Mel Ingber, Bellerose, New York; Charles C. Irby, Assistant Curator, Photographic Collections, The Gernsheim Collection, Humanities Research Center, University of Texas, Austin; Kling Photo Corp., Woodside, New York; David S. Lewandowski, Product Publicity Section, GAF Corp., New York; John W. Mathewson, Manager, General Sales, Herbick & Held Printing Co., Pittsburgh, Pennsylvania; Edward Murphy, Consumer Relations Department, Ehrenreich Photo-Optical Industries, Inc., Garden City, New York; Allan Porter, Editor, *Camera* magazine, Lucerne, Switzerland; William P. Ryan, Vice President, Calumet Manufacturing Co., Chicago, Illinois; Patricia Savoia and Elfriede Merman, The Manhattan Ballet School, New York City; Leonard Soned, New York City; William F. Swann, Manager, Professional, Commercial and Industrial Division, Eastman Kodak Co., Rochester, New York; John L. Tupper, Cousin's Island, Yarmouth, Maine; Robert Walch, Brooklyn, New York; Joel Snyder, Chicago, Illinois; David Vestal, Assoc. Editor, *Travel and Camera* and *Camera 35,* U.S. Camera Publishing Co., New York City; Peter Wehmann, Account Executive, Needham, Harper & Steers, Inc., New York City; Paul Wentz, Photographic Division, Honeywell, Inc., Long Island City, New York.

Picture Credits *Credits from left to right are separated by semicolons, from top to bottom by dashes.*

COVER—Harold Zipkowitz

Chapter 1: 11—Ken Kay. 12,13—Drawings by Pierre Haubensak. 14,15—Mt. Wilson Observatory—drawing by Virginia Wells —drawings by Pierre Haubensak. 16,17—Mt. Wilson Observatory; drawing by Pierre Haubensak; NASA. 18,19—Sun: Mt. Wilson Observatory; Earth: NASA, drawing by Pierre Haubensak; Harald Sund from Nancy Palmer. 20,21—Drawings by Pierre Haubensak; Harald Sund from Nancy Palmer. 22,23—Drawing by Pierre Haubensak; Harald Sund from Nancy Palmer. 24,25—Drawing by Pierre Haubensak; Jan Lukas. 27—Charles Harbutt © 1967 Magnum. 28—© Robert Gnant. 29—Irwin Dermer. 30,31 —Ray Metzker; Neal Slavin. 32—Harry Callahan. 33—Leonard Freed from Magnum. 34—Edward Weston, courtesy George Eastman House. 35 —Pierre Joussot. 36—© Harold Miller Null. 37 —© William Garnett. 38—George Krause. 39 —Frantisek Drtikol, courtesy of *Camera*. 40 —Kenneth Josephson. 41—Lars Werner Thieme. 42—Ronald Mesaros.

Chapter 2: 45—Courtesy Andre Jammes, Paris, Eddy van der Veen. 59—Courtesy the Metropolitan Museum of Art, New York City. 60,61—Joel Snyder. 62,63—Courtesy Smithsonian Institution, Paulus Leeser. 64,65 —Courtesy Cincinnati Public Library, The Longley Studio, Cincinnati—Courtesy George Eastman House. 66,67—Joel Snyder. 68,69 —Courtesy Jean Dieterle, Paris; from S.N.E.P. Illustration, © Baschet et Cie., Paris. 70 —Courtesy Smithsonian Institution. 71 —Courtesy Smithsonian Institution, Paulus Leeser. 72,73—Joel Snyder. 74—Courtesy Archives Photographiques, Bibliothèque Nationale, Paris. 75,76—Courtesy Smithsonian Institution, Paulus Leeser.

Chapter 3: 79—Collection Robert A. Weinstein, Los Angeles. 81—Staatliche Landesbildstelle, Hamburg. 82,83—Courtesy Gernsheim Collection, Humanities Research Center, University of Texas, Austin. 85—Copyright © 1966 by James D. Horan, Frank Lerner. 86,87 —Culver Pictures. 88,89—Courtesy Smithsonian Institution, National Anthropological Archives. 90 through 93—Courtesy Fondazione Primoli, Rome. 94—Courtesy Gernsheim Collection, Humanities Research Center, The University of Texas, Austin; courtesy George Eastman House (2). 95—Courtesy Gernsheim Collection, Humanities Research Center, The University of Texas, Austin, except top center, middle left and bottom right, courtesy George Eastman House. 97—Courtesy National Archives Records Group III. 98—Courtesy University of Pennsylvania, The Charles Van Pelt Library. 99—Courtesy New York Historical Society. 100,101—Courtesy Metropolitan Museum of Art; courtesy Library of Congress, Brady Collection. 102,103—Courtesy Metropolitan Museum of Art. 105—Courtesy C.P.R. Peacock, Derek Bayes. 106,107 —Courtesy Gernsheim Collection, Humanities Research Center, The University of Texas, Austin. 108—Courtesy Museum of Fine Arts, Copenhagen. 109—Courtesy Staatliche Landesbildstelle, Hamburg. 110,111 —Courtesy The Art Institute of Chicago. 112 through 118—Ernst Höltzer, courtesy Roland Hehn, Berlin.

Chapter 4: 121—Evelyn Hofer. 124—Drawings by Nicholas Fasciano. 125—Harold Zipkowitz —drawing by Nicholas Fasciano—Minor White. 126,127—Ken Kay except drawing by Jean Held. 128,129—Sebastian Milito. 130,131—Ann Douglass. 132,133—Leonard Soned—drawings by Jean Held. 134,135—Drawings by Nicholas Fasciano. 136,137—Evelyn Hofer. 139—Jeanloup Sieff. 140—Robert Lebeck. 141—Gary Renaud. 142,143—William Klein. 144,145—Mel Ingber. 146,147—Werner Köhler. 148,149— Minor White. 150,151—Marie Cosindas. 152—© Philippe Halsman.

Chapter 5: 155—Harold Zipkowitz; Mallory Battery Co., Frank Biondo. 158,159—Drawings by Nicholas Fasciano; Harold Zipkowitz. 160 —Ken Kay. 161—Ken Kay (4)—Henry Groskinsky (3). 162—Ken Kay. 163—Ken Kay (4)—Henry Groskinsky (3). 164—Drawing by John Svezia —Lou Carrano; Robert Walch and Lou Carrano. 165—Robert Walch. 166,167—Drawings by John Svezia; John Senzer. 168—Drawing by John Svezia; John Senzer. 169—Marcia Keegan. 171 —David Van Deveer, Marini, Climes and Guip, Inc. 172—Michael Semak. 173—Neal Slavin. 174 —Wilton Tifft. 175—Neal Slavin. 176—John Senzer—drawing by Pierre Haubensak. 177 —Drawings by Pierre Haubensak; Marcia Keegan—Leonard Soned. 178—Drawing by Pierre Haubensak—Leonard Soned.

Chapter 6: 181—Howard Harrison. 182,183 —Henry Groskinsky. 184—E. Gehri, Courtesy *Camera*. 185—Gary Renaud. 186 through 199 —Photographs by Henry Groskinsky, drawings by Nicholas Fasciano, except pages 190,191 —photographs by John Senzer. 192,193—Cat courtesy of Animal Talent Scouts. 198,199 —Dancer trained by The Manhattan Ballet School, New York City. 201,202,203—Ralph Morse. 205—Mark Kauffman. 206,207— Ralph Crane. 208,209—© Ben Rose. 210, 211—Neil Leifer for SPORTS ILLUSTRATED. 212—Yale Joel. 213—Ralph Morse. 214,215 —© Arnold Newman. 216,217—Drawing by Nicholas Fasciano; George Silk. 218,219 —Drawing by Nicholas Fasciano; Fritz Goro. 220—Lennart Nilsson.

Index
Numerals in italics indicate a photograph, painting or drawing of the subject mentioned.

Printed in U.S.A.